The Darrell Survey

Golf Equipment
ALMANAC 2004

A Consumer Resource

The latest golf-equipment data
from Consumer Surveys and
the Professional Tours

DARRELL SURVEY COMPANY

To Harry C. and others...
who live, breathe & love Golf

Acknowledgments

We are pleased to present the fifth edition of the GOLF EQUIPMENT ALMANAC, marking another milestone in the eight-decade history of THE DARRELL SURVEY. 30,000 face-to-face surveys a year are no small task, yet our indefatiguable staff gets the job done.

The ALMANAC is produced by Mark F. Schwartz, André Burke and Lonnie Peralta. Graphics designed by Don Tinling; statistical modeling provided by Doss Struse.

For DARRELL SURVEY: Ibrahim Mesallem, Delia St. Pierre, Alex Roytman, Coreen Peralta, Robert Duffy, Malcolm Heber, Lois Peralta, Zayra Cabot, Ken Habib and Tina Madden. Consumer analysis software by Sergey Glouschak and his team. Thanks to Mark Agnello, PGA Tour Information Systems, for his help with Tour statistical data.

Our terrific tournament surveyors include Evelyn Merrin, Alison Hellwege, Diane Scott, Chuck Carroll, Buff White, Sara Johnson, Steve Parker, Kathy Hartman, Blair Philip, Shigeaki "Leon" & Fumiyo Kameshima (with help from Kyoko & Genki Nagata), Julie Randolph, Monica Bertsch, Betty Portilla, Karen Widener, Jenny Miller, Patti Inman, Martha Baker, Carol Daley, Ashley Buha, Stephanie Sterling, Heather Gove and Heather Peterson.

Our roster of surveyors emeritus include Sarah Strange, Jeanine Morgan, Sue Bryant, Jan Rose, Linda Leslie, Shelly Norris, Jane Betley, Jill Rintoul, Julie Eger, Suzi Johnson, Stephanie Rowen, Annie Ives, Ashley Langham, Holly Hallet, Beth Fabel, Cissye Gallagher, Julia Hnatiuk, Kimberly Gay, Kathy Heinen, Norma McKeever, Gina Shea, Beryl O'Neil, Lori Legatt and Lisa Peterson.

Never far from our memories are Ruby Palmer, Eddie McKeever, and Eddie and Virginia Darrell.

Finally, our love and thanks to Anthony, Mary, Ann Nicole, Bruno and Biff; Jake, Beau and Debra; and our mother, Kathleen.

SUSAN M. NAYLOR AND JOHN MINKLEY

THE DARRELL SURVEY

Table of Contents

Table of Contents

1963

Arnold Palmer and Eddie Darrell

A Letter from Arnold Palmer

I turned professional in 1954 and won my first PGA Tour event in 1955. I can't remember playing professional golf when the Darrell Survey wasn't part of it.

Eddie was this round little man who was always standing with a book and pen writing down the equipment he observed. He cared about getting things right. If he thought a player showed him one ball on the first tee, but switched to another ball on the course, he would be out there checking with his binoculars to make sure.

Eddie and his wife Virginia worked hard to give the Darrell Survey what it has never surrendered – credibility. For the last twenty-five years Susan Naylor and her brother John Minkley have continued this tradition of accuracy and integrity with their own sets of binoculars.

I have always loved golf clubs, and I believe that having an exact record of all this is invaluable – it is part of golf's rich history. The Darrell Survey has long been the historian of golf equipment, working hard to get things right.

With all the changes in golf, it's nice to know that the people behind the Darrell Survey haven't changed. They still go about their job in a quiet, understated way. I'll bet most spectators don't even know what they're doing out there on the first tee.

Eddie isn't around anymore, but the Darrell Survey still reflects his philosophy of getting the job done without getting in the way. I can still picture Eddie, looking in everybody's bag, writing down his notes like he was some kind of detective.

This is part of golf's grand heritage, and I'm happy to say it's still here.

ARNOLD PALMER

Introduction

Some shop owners do not like this book, and would rather that you don't know about it. But here it is in your hands.

A friend of ours didn't have an ALMANAC. Not too long ago, he purchased a driver. We asked him why he chose that particular model. Well,

Eddie Darrell and his Tourney Car

the clerk at the local golf discount store had told him it was a leading driver on the Champions Tour.

We took out the most recent ALMANAC—and there was no mention of this brand on the Champions Tour driver page. To make certain, we looked back a couple more years using previous editions, but in three years, the driver had never been used by a single Senior player. How could we know for certain? Because every club brand used on Tour is listed in this book.

Our friend, though disappointed with his driver, was happy to become the owner of a complete set of Almanacs, 2000 to the present.

Rapidly evolving technology and dazzling marketing are sweeping the sport of golf, with magazines, websites, salespeople, friends and everyone else offering advice on equpment.

Payne Stewart & Susan Naylor

This book is a respite from the whirlwind. We don't offer any advice. We present you with the facts, providing a "double check" on any information you may have heard, as well as the broader perspective of what your fellow golfers, and pros around the world, are up to.

Amid all the hype, these numbers speak for themselves.

Arnold Palmer & Susan Naylor

When we created the ALMANAC, we wanted it to be helpful to golfers at all levels of expertise — not an easy task. For example, low-handicap players might be bored by the questions a newcomer to the game might ask.

Our answer was to put as much detail into the book as possible. This way, neophytes can get the big picture quickly, while certified golf nuts can wallow in the fine details, like knowing every single model used to win tournaments each year.

In this year's edition, we have added data for the Nationwide Tour for the first time. Equipment enthusiasts will enjoy studying the equipment differences between PGA and Nationwide Tours.

Meanwhile, high-handicap players will find plenty of information regarding equipment that's right for them.

And anyone can pick up this book, begin reading at any chapter, and learn a fact or two to "talk a good game."

We hope our readers will continue to collect the annual ALMANACS, creating a history of golf equipment right on your bookshelves. With this, our fifth edition, the era when only the big golf manufacturers had access to THE DARRELL SURVEY is firmly in the past.

Thanks for your support, and, as always, "You can count on us to count for you!"

SUSAN MINKLEY NAYLOR

JOHN MINKLEY

The Darrell Survey

T he Darrell Survey observes the equipment used by professional golfers at tournaments and reports its findings to golf manufacturers.

Currently, the Darrell Survey covers **more than 200 tournaments** each season on the PGA, Champions, LPGA and Nationwide Tours, the Japan Golf Tour and the British Open, as well as selected USGA and NCAA events. At the opening tee on the first day of play, our surveyor teams inspect the bag of every player, reporting on usage of clubs, balls, shirts, shoes, spikes, shafts, grips and headgear.

The Darrell Survey has also performed **extensive consumer research** over the last 23 years, visiting public and private golf courses around the country to observe what recreational golfers are using and to ask them what they think about it.

With the ALMANAC, the Darrell Survey presents a yearly summary of consumer and professional-tour data. The statistics that golf manufacturers have relied upon for decades are now available for golf enthusiasts everywhere.

History

I n the 1930s, A.J. Spalding & Brothers hired **Eddie Darrell** to tour the United States with some of the best golfers of the day. The goal: to promote the Scottish game of golf, and to standardize the way it was being played in America. At their exhibition games, Eddie would announce the shots over the public address system, then pack up the players' equipment in the Spalding truck and head on to the next town.

As tournament golf developed in the U.S., Eddie started an **official weekly report** of the equipment that the players were using... and the "Darrell Survey" was born.

Eddie and his wife Virginia carried on the survey until 1980, when they turned the company over to Susan Naylor, their longtime family friend and employee, and her brother John Minkley.

Thus, the Darrell Survey has been a **family-owned company** and a tradition of golf for more than 70 years.

The Nature of this Book

The DARRELL SURVEY ALMANAC will not give you a **critique** or an **analysis** of the brands or models, nor will it give a recommendation of any particular model. It will only relate the actual usage shares and consumer opinions—as a famous fictional police detective used to say, "Just the facts."

Many people are curious about the equipment that **particular pro golfers** use on the Tour. The Darrell Survey compiles such information for in-house use by golf manufacturers, but does not release it to the public. The data used in the Almanac reveals trends without divulging the private information of specific players.

Whenever this book does make statements about individual players, it is because the golfer has officially **endorsed** that brand or product during the year of play cited. For example, the list of 2003 Tournament Winners includes the **bag affiliation** of each player because the bag logo indicates an official endorsement on the part of the touring pro.

The Darrell Survey has long worked to protect the rights of players and will continue to do so.

Some Browsing Ideas

* You can **study** the Almanac to help you with your next golf purchase, or to plan ahead for your equipment needs.

* **Browse** through it and find a wealth of interesting facts and trivia about what the pros are using.

* **Look up your own equipment** and see how it fares in the Darrell Golfer Satisfaction Ratings™.

* Check out the tour data, which is **all inclusive**. Every brand used on the PGA, Champions, Nationwide, LPGA or Japan Golf Tours in 2003 is listed.

* Study the PGA Tour **player performance statistics** to get a feel for how the equipment fares in the hands of the world's top golfers.

How the Almanac is Organized

Throughout the year, the DARRELL SURVEY gathers information about golf equipment by three main methods—the **Consumer Usage Report**, the **Consumer Satisfaction Surveys**, and the **Professional Tour Reports.** From these primary sources, highlights of the data have been summarized in the DARRELL SURVEY ALMANAC for easy reference.

❖ Consumer Usage Report:

- Brands and models seen most frequently in use by recreational golfers across the country.

- How this usage breaks down by *handicap* and *age (see chart, next page.)*

❖ Consumer Satisfaction Surveys:

- Golf equipment rated by the people who use it.

- Ratings of brands and models by handicap and age.

- Ratings of brands and models according to specific criteria such as *value, appearance, accuracy, fit.*

The value of each brand and model is listed on the bar on a scale of 500 *(see chart, next page.)* For more information on satisfaction ratings, please see page 11.

❖ Professional Tours:

- All brands of equipment used by players on the PGA, Champions, Nationwide, LPGA and Japan Tours.

- The brands and models that have the *most wins.*

The tour data is all inclusive. **Every brand** used on the tour is listed in the tour charts.

Chapter by Chapter:
Usage, Opinions & Tours

The illustrations *below* correspond to the text on the *opposite page*. The **tabs** on the edge of each right-hand page in the book indicate the chapter and subsection you are in, for easy reference.

Consumer Usage

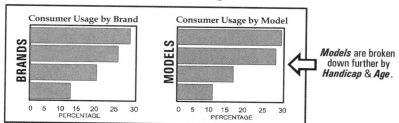

Models are broken down further by **Handicap** & **Age**.

Consumer Opinions

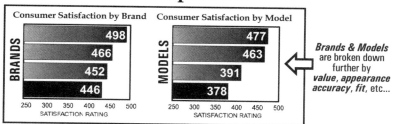

Brands & Models are broken down further by **value, appearance accuracy, fit**, etc...

Professional Usage

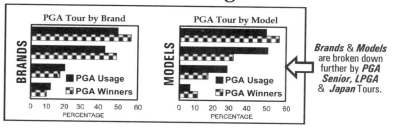

Brands & **Models** are broken down further by **PGA Senior, LPGA** & **Japan** Tours.

In addition: PGA Tour Performance Statistics, included at the end of the Ball, Driver and Putter chapters.

Examples of How to Use the Almanac

The Almanac is **not just for golf fanatics**, although even the most know-ledgable golfer can learn from it.

Because of the depth of information available, the book may seem daunting at first glance. But each page stands on its own. Just dive in and **browse anywhere you like.**

A **non-golfer**, a **beginner** or even a **scratch player** can learn something about equipment on each page of this Almanac. This book empowers consumers to ask intelligent questions when shopping for new equipment for themselves or for a gift.

The charts below provide ideas for **navigating** through the book.

You're looking to buy a box of balls for a college-age player.

College Player	Look up:	By Brand	By Model
Equipment....Ball	Consumer Ball Usage................................Page 4............Page 5		
Handicap........4	Ball Usage by Handicap (0-10)................Page 6............Page 7		
	Ball Satisfaction by Handicap (0-10)....Page 12............Page 13		
Age................20	Ball Usage by Age (>30).........................Page 8............Page 9		
	Ball Satisfaction by Age (>30)..............Page 14 ....Page 15		
Tour.................NCAA	Amateur Ball Usage - NCAA Tour.......................Page 19		
Factor............Distance	Ball Satisfaction Ratings/Distance............Page 16.........Page 17		

You're la 65 year old dad who's a 12 handicap looking to try a new driver.

Father	Look up:	By Brand	By Model
Equipment.....DRIVER	Consumer Driver Usage...........................Page 84............Page 85		
Handicap........12	Driver Usage by Handicap (11-20)........................Page 86		
	Driver Satisfaction by Handicap (11-20)...Page 90............Page 91		
Age................65	Driver Usage by Age (51+)...................................Page 87		
	Driver Satisfaction by Age (51+)..............Page 92............Page 93		
Tour.................SENIOR	Pro Driver Usage - Champions Tour.......Page 100.........Page 101		

BALLS

Chapter 1

Callaway HX

Once again this year, the **Titeist Pro V1** family of balls is the predominant choice among professionals and consumer golfers alike, continuing its resounding success in the face of new models from technologically savvy competitors.

On the **PGA Tour** alone, the Pro V1, including the Star and Diamond models, won more than $142 million dollars during the 2003 season *(page 33)*.

Low-handicap consumers join the pros in choosing the Pro V1 *(page 7)*. And three varieties of Pro V1 are found in the top five highest-rated models for **golfer satisfaction** *(page 17)*.

Of course, other balls have their fans on Tour. Among the pros' top picks are the **Callaway HX** models, **Nike Tour Accuracy II Long, Maxfli M3 Tour 432, Nike One, Hogan Apex Tour, Strata Tour Ace, Precept U-Tri Tour** and **Wilson True Tour Elite** *(pages 21 to 31)*.

Titleist Pro V1

The **PGA Performance Statistics** on pages 32-33 show impressive **driving distance** results for the Nike One and One TW, Maxfli M3 Tour 432, Callaway HX Tour, Srixon Hi Brid Tour and Titleist Pro V1x.

For **driving accuracy,** the PGA pros averaged highest with the regular Titleist Pro V1, Precept U-Tri, Hogan Apex Tour, Nike One and One TW, and Wilson True Tour Elite.

BALLS: OVERVIEW

Low-handicap consumer golfers are likely to follow the lead of the pros when choosing their ball, but higher handicaps are happy to choose balls from a lower price range, or models that are designed specifically for the their level of the game.

Page 7 shows a world of difference between lower handicap consumers, who use the Pro V1s and the Strata Tour, and the higher handicaps, who favor Top-Flite XL 2000, Precept MC Lady and Titleist NXT.

So the higher handicap ALMANAC reader might pay particular attention to the satisfaction ratings of like-skilled golfers, broken down on page 13.

Top-Flite XL 2000

For more information on how Darrell Survey consumer satisfaction ratings are scored, please see page 11.

MAXFLI Noodle

In 2003, DARRELL SURVEY conducted 23,412 person-to-person, on-course pro surveys on the PGA, Champions, LPGA, Nationwide and Japan Golf Tours as well as at major amateur events and the British Open.

Our **consumer** research was expanded to include additional surveys during the winter months, in order to better track the fast-moving golf marketplace. U.S. consumer usage and satisfaction data was gathered through over **6,000 interviews**, person-to-person, at public and private golf courses across America.

So in this dense chapter, you're getting the whole story on balls. With nearly 30,000 surveys backing up this year's data, THE DARRELL SURVEY is pleased to keep you up to date.

Precept Lady

Read carefully and decide for yourself!

Consumer Ball Usage by Brand*

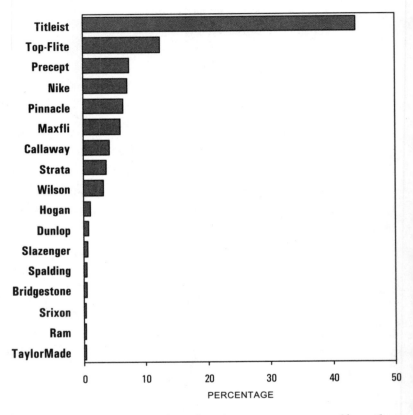

This chart shows that more than four in ten consumer golfers play **Titleist** balls.

These are **not sales figures**, but what you see if you go out on the course and actually count what people are using—which is, of course, exactly what we did.

*This year's Almanac separates out distinct brands, even though they may be made by the same manufacturer. Recent acquisitions and licensing agreements in the marketplace have made it impractical to list our data by manufacturer rather than by the brand name appearing on the equipment or packaging.

Thus, **Maxfli** and **TaylorMade** appear separately, as do **Titleist** and **Pinnacle**; **Callaway, Top-Flite, Ben Hogan** and **Strata**.

Consumer Ball Usage by Model

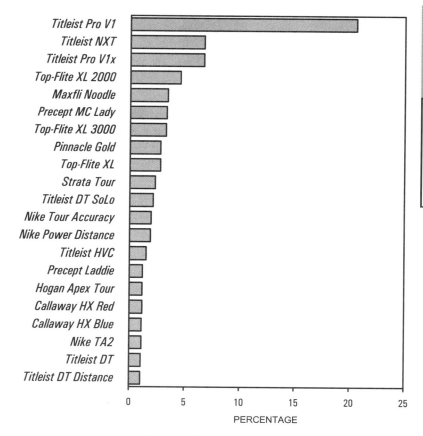

Percentage share of consumer equipment in use. Nationwide on-course consumer survey conducted summer 2003; 3,264 respondents.

For the third year running, the Titleist Pro V1 is the most commonly used consumer ball.

Many models seen here are quite different from those found in pro usage *(see pages 22)*.

Our survey measures usage, not sales. These are the ball brands actually used *on the course* by the frequent, relatively serious golfers who constitute our consumer survey base. For more information, see the *Survey Methodology* at the end of this book.

Ball Brand Usage by Handicap

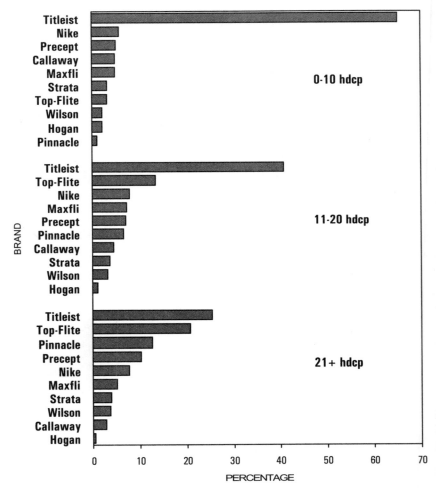

Percentage share of consumer equipment in use. Nationwide on-course consumer survey conducted summer 2003; 3,264 respondents.

Clearly, low-handicap golfers are devoted to Titleist.

As seen in the model breakdown, *opposite page,* the ball market for higher-handicap consumers is actually quite competitive, with no one model dominating—in stark contrast to the low-handicaps.

Ball Model Usage by Handicap

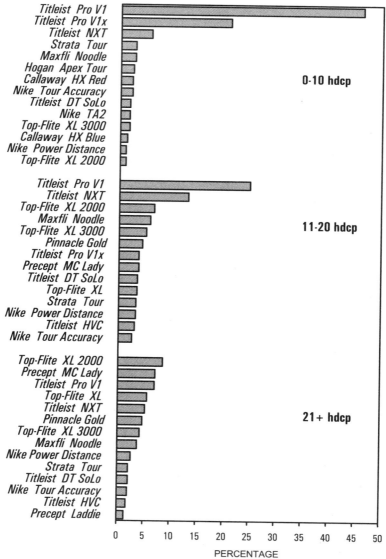

Percentage share of consumer equipment in use. Nationwide on-course
consumer survey conducted summer 2003; 3,264 respondents.

Ball Brand Usage by Age

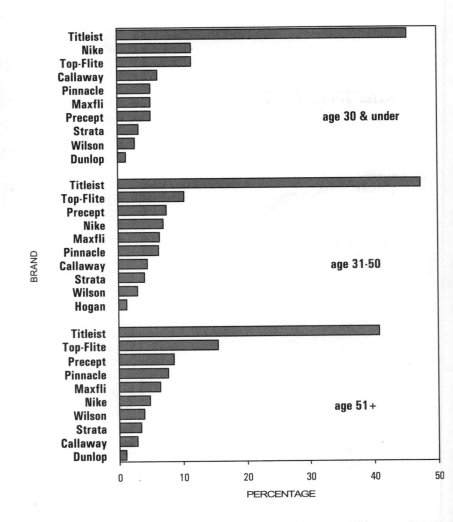

Percentage share of consumer equipment in use. Nationwide on-course consumer survey conducted summer 2003; 3,203 respondents.

While Titleist dominates all age groups, Nike makes a big breakthrough this year, becoming the number two ball among young golfers.

Ball Model Usage by Age

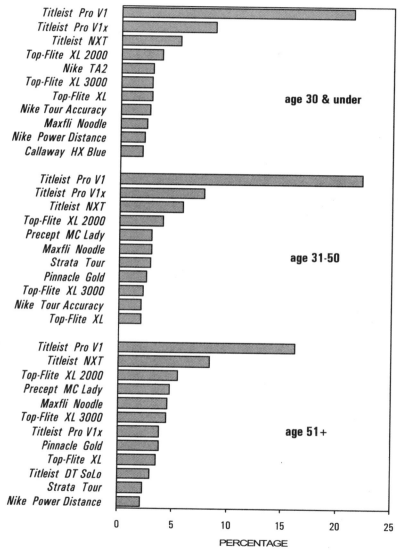

Percentage share of consumer equipment in use. Nationwide on-course consumer survey conducted summer 2003; 3,203 respondents.

BALLS: CLOSE UP

Iron Byron Gets a Makeover

All ball models are tested by the **U.S. Golf Association**. All balls must meet certain requirements. Balls that are too hot, or too long, are labeled **nonconforming** and cannot be used in tournament play.

Balls are restricted in **initial velocity** and **overall distance**. Under a proposed change in the rules, which is expected to go into effect in June, 2004, balls will be allowed to travel a total distance (carry and roll, under normal conditions) of **320 yards**.

For the past 20 years, the maximum overall distance has been 296.8 yards. Now it will be increased by 23.2 yards.

Why? Because the USGA has **changed its test procedures**. When the overall distance standard was adopted in 1984, balls were tested with the **Iron Byron** mechanical robot. Named after legendary golfer Byron Nelson, the robot swung a wooden-headed driver at 109 miles an hour. These parameters have gone unchanged for two decades.

Now the USGA has replaced Iron Byron's wooden driver with a **modern titanium driver** (it still has a steel shaft, however). Furthermore, the clubhead speed has been increased to **120 mph**.

So the corresponding overall distance has gone up to 320 yards. This sounds like a big number, but the USGA says **nothing will change**. The same balls will be conforming, and newly developed balls will not carry or roll any longer than the old ones did for ordinary golfers.

The new test causes the balls to go farther, but the balls themselves are still the same. Turns out there are still no magic bullets in the shooting game called golf.

What are the Darrell Survey Golfer Satisfaction Ratings?

How satisfied are you? How do you rate your equipment for value, distance, spin, feel, accuracy, durability and forgiveness?

We ask these questions thousands of times a year, of golfers just like you. We compile their answers into the DARRELL SURVEY GOLFER SATISFACTION RATINGS™.

The ratings come from consumer golfers who are **actually using the brands and models in question on the day of the survey.** This is not a theoretical focus group, club test or "what if" study... these are real people using their own real equipment.

500 is the top score on the rating scale. Because golfers are assessing equipment they have chosen to play, scores can be quite high. **Differences of only a few points are not statistically significant.**

Golfers rate each piece of equipment for individual attributes such as value and accuracy, and then for overall satisfaction.

To appear in the ALMANAC, a brand or model must have **sufficient sample size**, and must also rank within the **top echelon of scores** for the category in question. But because a brand or model might not appear solely because of insufficient sample size, **the absence of any brand or model does not necessarily indicate a low score**.

Unlike Darrell Survey usage data, the Golfer Satisfaction Ratings are **opinions**, which can have different statistical properties. For example, smaller brands with only a few popular models may outscore larger brands that have more users and a wide variety of models. *(Each brand score represents an average of all models.)*

Sometimes a brand or model may appear on one satisfaction chart but not another. This can be due to a lack of adequate sample size for that brand or model; for example, iron models geared to low-handicap players don't have enough usage to receive a rating from the higher-handicap players surveyed.

So if you don't see a score for your model, it may have received a low rating. Or it may not have had enough users to be rated accurately. **Use all the data in this book** to get the complete picture.

Darrell Golfer Satisfaction Ratings™
Ball Brands by Handicap

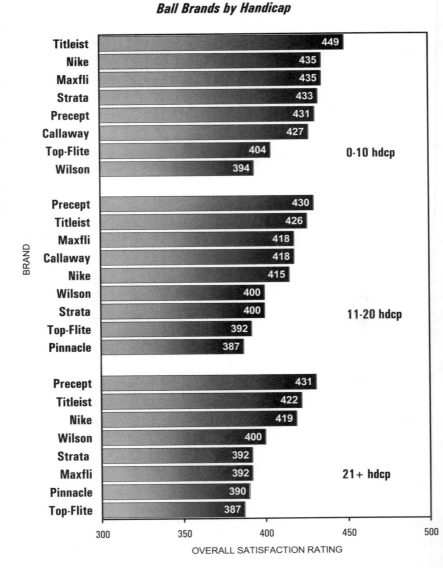

"How satisfied are you with your equipment?" 500 is most satisfied. 100 is least satisfied. Consumer golfers rate the equipment they are actually using the day of the survey. 2,265 opinion respondents. (Minimum of 15 responses per subgroup for brands/models shown.)

BALLS: CONSUMER OPINIONS

Darrell Golfer Satisfaction Ratings™
Ball Models by Handicap

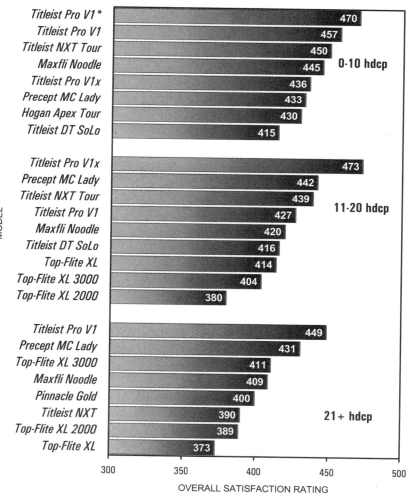

Balls

Consumer Opinions

MODEL

0-10 hdcp

- Titleist Pro V1 * — 470
- Titleist Pro V1 — 457
- Titleist NXT Tour — 450
- Maxfli Noodle — 445
- Titleist Pro V1x — 436
- Precept MC Lady — 433
- Hogan Apex Tour — 430
- Titleist DT SoLo — 415

11-20 hdcp

- Titleist Pro V1x — 473
- Precept MC Lady — 442
- Titleist NXT Tour — 439
- Titleist Pro V1 — 427
- Maxfli Noodle — 420
- Titleist DT SoLo — 416
- Top-Flite XL — 414
- Top-Flite XL 3000 — 404
- Top-Flite XL 2000 — 380

21+ hdcp

- Titleist Pro V1 — 449
- Precept MC Lady — 431
- Top-Flite XL 3000 — 411
- Maxfli Noodle — 409
- Pinnacle Gold — 400
- Titleist NXT — 390
- Top-Flite XL 2000 — 389
- Top-Flite XL — 373

OVERALL SATISFACTION RATING

"How satisfied are you with your equipment?" 500 is most satisfied.
100 is least satisfied.   2,265 opinion respondents. (Minimum of 12
responses per subgroup for brands/models shown.)

Differences of only a few rating points are not statistically significant.

Note that better golfers generally rate their equipment more favorably than less skilled players.

Darrell Golfer Satisfaction Ratings™
Ball Brands by Age

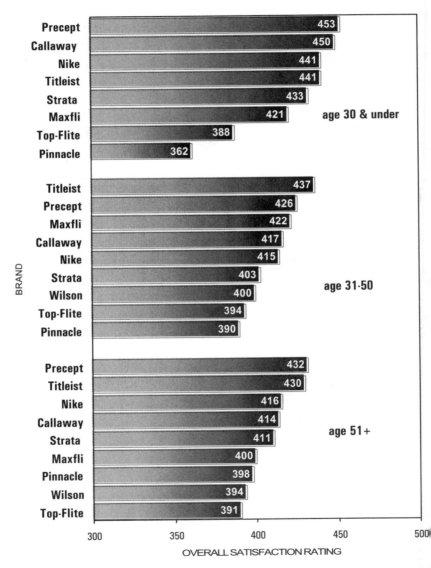

BRAND

age 30 & under	
Precept	453
Callaway	450
Nike	441
Titleist	441
Strata	433
Maxfli	421
Top-Flite	388
Pinnacle	362

age 31-50	
Titleist	437
Precept	426
Maxfli	422
Callaway	417
Nike	415
Strata	403
Wilson	400
Top-Flite	394
Pinnacle	390

age 51+	
Precept	432
Titleist	430
Nike	416
Callaway	414
Strata	411
Maxfli	400
Pinnacle	398
Wilson	394
Top-Flite	391

OVERALL SATISFACTION RATING

"How satisfied are you with your equipment?" 500 is most satisfied. 100 is least satisfied. 2,265 opinion respondents. (Minimum of 15 responses per subgroup for brands/models shown.)

Darrell Golfer Satisfaction Ratings™
Ball Models by Age

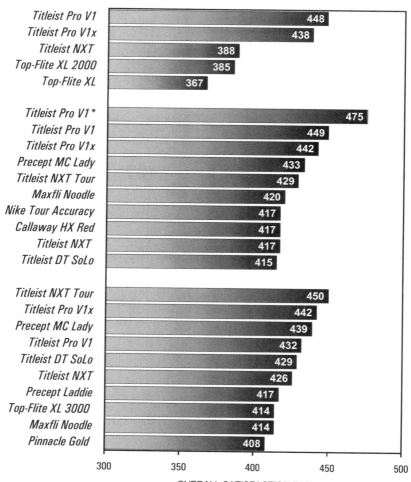

OVERALL SATISFACTION RATING

How satisfied are you with your equipment?" 500 is most satisfied. 100 is least satisfied. 2,265 opinion respondents. (Minimum of 10 responses per subgroup for brands/models shown.)

Titleist models grab the highest satisfaction ratings from every age group.

As seen *opposite*, Precept scores well on a brand-wide basis.

BALLS: CONSUMER OPINIONS

Darrell Golfer Satisfaction Ratings™
Ball Brands by Feature

—— Satisfaction SCORE by Equipment Feature ——

BALLS

(Listed Alphabetically)	Overall	Distance	Accuracy	Feel	Durability	Value	Spin
Average Score	420	427	419	424	419	413	407
Callaway	*423*	*431*	*431*	*433*	*424*	412	*418*
Dunlop	*429*	414	414	419	*433*	*443*	*410*
Hogan	*443*	*456*	*456*	*460*	*421*	*425*	*454*
Maxfli	413	413	413	*423*	412	*417*	401
Nike	421	*420*	*420*	415	412	411	399
Pinnacle	391	383	383	378	408	412	362
Precept	*431*	*428*	*428*	*440*	*428*	*428*	*418*
Strata	412	407	407	414	404	403	*402*
Titleist	*435*	*435*	*435*	*443*	*429*	412	*425*
Top-Flite	392	387	387	387	407	412	375
Wilson	399	396	396	392	397	408	375

"How satisfied are you with your equipment?" 500 is most satisfied. 100 is least satisfied. 2,265 opinion respondents. (Minimum of 15 responses per subgroup for brands shown.)

❖ Compare each score to the average seen in the top row.

❖ Numbers in ***bold italic*** indicate top 5 scores in each category.

❖ Scores for individual models are listed on the opposite page.

As seen on the opposite page, a number of **Titleist** models as well as the **Hogan** Apex Tour ball receive top satisfaction ratings from recreational golfers.

Maxfli's A10, Callaway's HX Blue and the Precept Laddie receive Top Five scores in selected categories.

The models represented onthe opposite page have overall scores of more than 400. Any models with lower scores do not appear on the chart.

BALLS: CONSUMER OPINIONS

Darrell Golfer Satisfaction Ratings™
Ball Models by Feature

—— Satisfaction SCORE by Equipment Feature ——

BALLS

(Listed Alphabetically)	Overall	Distance	Accuracy	Feel	Durability	Value	Spin
Average Score	*420*	*427*	*419*	*424*	*419*	*413*	*407*
Callaway CB1	423	423	423	408	*438*	*446*	415
Callaway HX Blue	425	*450*	442	*458*	417	408	433
Callaway HX Red	415	415	420	420	410	400	415
Callaway Rule 35	415	438	431	423	415	392	408
Hogan Apex Tour	*445*	*450*	*464*	*468*	419	429	*452*
Maxfli A10	433	446	*446*	438	*446*	423	*446*
Maxfli Noodle	420	417	414	425	415	427	396
Maxfli Revolution	420	420	433	433	403	413	*440*
Nike Power Distance	432	442	421	426	416	411	395
Nike TA2	430	445	435	430	425	410	415
Nike Tour Accuracy	422	422	417	417	417	433	411
Pinnacle Gold	402	407	400	391	411	419	377
Precept Laddie	426	435	430	443	*443*	*452*	426
Precept MC Lady	435	433	423	435	431	435	408
Strata Tour Ace	433	411	417	433	417	394	428
Titleist DT	426	430	425	437	432	429	407
Titleist DT SoLo	421	423	423	438	426	434	387
Titleist HP	423	431	408	408	*455*	*450*	425
Titleist HVC	*450*	442	433	*450*	433	*458*	*442*
Titleist NXT Distance	425	433	417	417	433	*442*	400
Titleist NXT Tour	433	433	434	443	429	431	414
Titleist Pro V1	*444*	*451*	*444*	*457*	433	408	437
Titleist Pro V1 *	*467*	*462*	*471*	*476*	*460*	433	*476*
Titleist Pro V1x	*442*	*471*	*455*	*450*	424	407	435

"How satisfied are you with your equipment?" 500 is most satisfied. 100 is least satisfied. 2,265 opinion respondents. (Minimum of 12 responses per subgroup for brands/models shown.)

Some of the highly ranked models seen here are not seen on pages 13 and 15 due to sample sizes that are not large enough to generate statistically reliable results by handicap or age.

The Pro V1* receives the highest score of any model in every category except *distance* and *value*.

Buy the Dozen

Periodically the USGA collects balls from players at big tournaments. The balls are tested to make sure the pros are not using souped-up balls.

The Royal & Ancient Golf Club of St. Andrews, Scotland, sanctions all USGA ball tests, and the two ruling bodies have produced a joint set of rules that apply to golf balls around the world.

The bottom line: golf balls are tightly regulated, and all of them must meet very strict manufacturing standards.

Top Ball Models
At Major Amateur Events

U.S. AMATEUR
Titleist Pro V1x
Titleist Pro V1
Precept U-Tri Tour
Callaway HX Red
Nike TA2 LNG
Hogan Apex Tour
Nike TA2 SPN
Titleist NXT Tour

U.S. WOMEN'S AMATEUR
Titleist Pro V1
Titleist Pro V1x
Callaway HX Red
Callaway CTU 30 Red
Nike TA2 LNG
Nike TA2 SPN
Titleist Pro V1 Star

NCAA DIV. 1 MEN'S
Titleist Pro V1x
Titleist Pro V1
Precept U-Tri Tour
Nike TA2 LNG
Nike TA2 SPN
Precept Tour Premium LS

NCAA WOMEN'S
Titleist Pro V1
Titleist Pro V1x
Nike TA2 LNG
Callaway HX Red
Nike Tour Accuracy DD
Maxfli M3 Tour
Callaway HX Blue

U.S. BOYS JUNIOR
Titleist Pro V1x
Titleist Pro V1
Callaway CTU 30 Red
Hogan Apex Tour

U.S. GIRLS JUNIOR
Titleist Pro V1
Titleist Pro V1x
Callaway HX Red
Callaway CTU 30 Red
Maxfli Noodle

2003 data. Listed in order of decreasing usage at each tournament.

These tournaments are major national amateur events, played by the top young players in the United States.

In addition to the Pro V1, an array of Callaway, Precept, Nike, Hogan and Maxfli models are used by top amateur golfers.

Balls

Amateur Usage

Life Begins at 40?

Perhaps the most interesting development on the 2003 PGA Tour was the flabergasting number of tournaments, 15, won by players who were **40 or older.**

The Tour does not keep complete age records, but this is believed to easily be a record. A total of 11 players over age 40 won 15 times.

The rundown: **Kenny Perry**, 42, won three times. **Vijay Singh** also won three times after turning 40 in February. Singh won a fourth tournament less than a month before his 40th birthday.

The other **fortysomethings** who won Tour events in 2003 were Craig Stadler (50), Peter Jacobsen (49), Scott Hoch (47), Bob Tway (44), Tommy Armour III (43), J.L. Lewis (43), Fred Couples (43), John Huston (42) and Kirk Triplett (41).

Three other players in their 40s—Nick Price, Brad Faxon and Jay Haas—didn't win but still managed to finish among the **top 20** on the money list. Overall, 10 of the top 31 spots were claimed by golfers who were at least 40.

The trend continued on the **LPGA Tour**, where Beth Daniel, Juli Inkster, Rosie Jones and Meg Mallon were over-40 winners.

Possible explanations for this phenomenon: Today's veteran players are in **better physical condition** than players in the past, these players are more **highly motivated** to beat the younger stars, and **modern equipment** allows golfers to fine-tune their games in a more precise manner.

BALLS: PRO USAGE

Tour - Ball by Brand

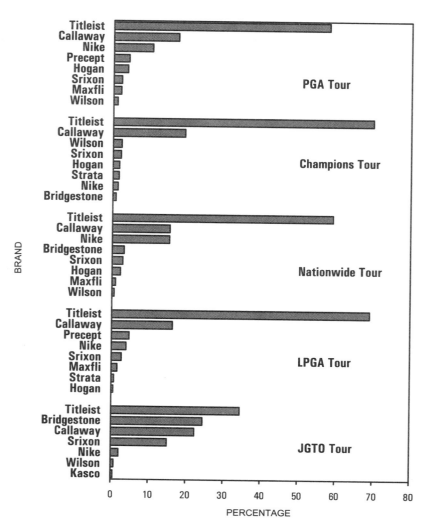

All 2003 Tournaments.

Titleist, Callaway and **Nike** balls lead on the U.S. Tours, joined in Japan by the **Bridgestone** (Precept) and **Srixon** brands.

PGA Tour - Balls by Brand
Overall vs. Winners

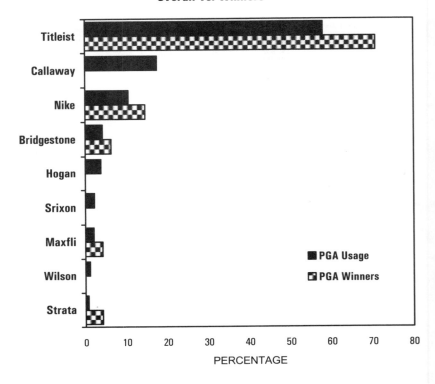

All 2003 PGA Tournaments. Sample size: 6,305 players; 48 winners.

All the winning PGA Tour players used **Titleist, Nike, Bridgestone, Maxfli** or **Strata** balls in 2003, as seen in the patterned bars above.

Titleist Pro V1 and **Pro V1x** balls account fo the vast majority of all PGA Tour wins *(opposite page)*.

Other than scoring victories, how do the balls perform for the pros? Please see the PGA statistical breakdown starting on page 30, including **driving distance, driving accuracy**, and **official money won**.

Bridgestone Sports markets its equipment in the U.S. under the **Precept** and the new **TourStage** brand labels.

PGA Tour - Balls by Model
Overall vs. Winners

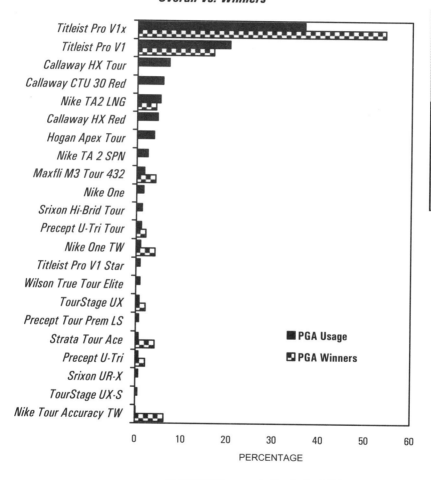

All 2003 PGA Tournaments. Sample size: 6,503w players; 48 winners. Every model used to win a tournament is on this chart.

Over half of all balls used on the PGA Tour in 2003 were from the
Titleist ProV1 series.

Three different **Nike** models, the *TA2 LNG*, the *One TW* and the *Tour
Accuracy TW*, were use to win PGA tournaments in 2003.

Champions Tour - Balls by Brand
Overall vs. Winners

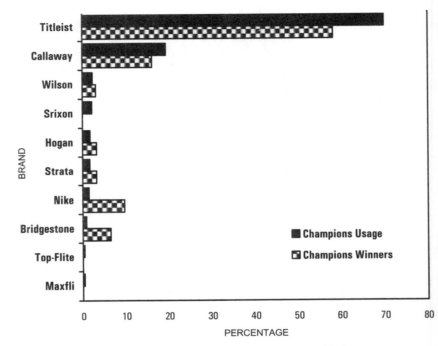

All 2003 Champions Tournaments. Sample size: 2,605 players; 33 winners.
Every model used to win a tournament is on this chart.

More than 7 in 10 senior players use **Titleist.**

Five other ball brands also had Champions Tour winners in 2003: **Callaway**, **Nike**, **Precept/Bridgestone**, **Hogan**, **Strata** and **Wilson.**

You can cross-reference staff players with the wins identified above by checking out the complete list of 2003 tournament winners at the end of Chapter 7.

Champions Tour - Balls by Model
Overall vs. Winners

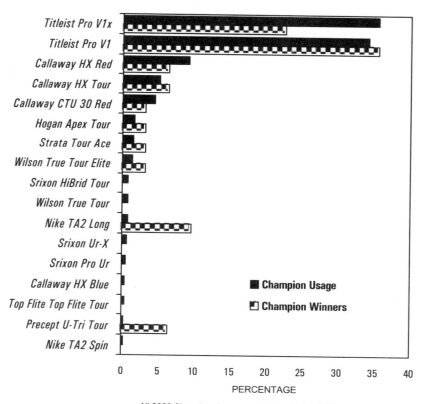

All 2003 Champions Tournaments. Sample size: 2,605 players; 31 winners. Every model used to win a tournament is on this chart.

Titleist's Pro V1x edges out the **Pro V1** in usage, but the Pro V1 captures more wins.

Callaway's HX and **CTU** models also have a strong following among the Senior players, while **Nike's TA2 LNG** model is responsible for three wins.

Nationwide Tour - Balls by Brand
Overall vs. Winners

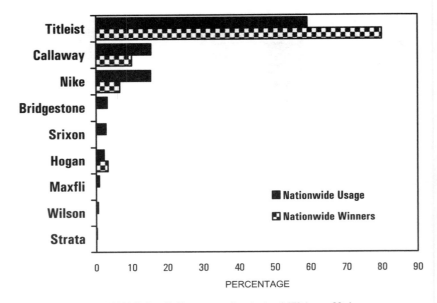

All 2003 Nationwide Tournaments. Sample size: 4,476players; 30winners.
Every model used to win a tournament is on this chart.

On the 2003 **Nationwide Tour**, **Titleist** balls contributed to 80% of all wins.

This year we put data from the Nationwide Tour in the Almanac for the first time.

Equipment data from the Nationwide Tour is not available in any other publication.

Nationwide Tour - Balls by Model
Overall vs. Winners

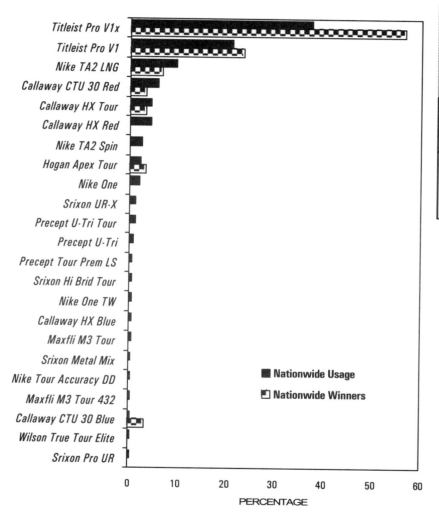

All 2003 Nationwide Tournaments. Sample size: 4,476players; 30winners.

Every model used to win a tournament is on this chart

BALLS: PRO USAGE

LPGA Tour - Balls by Brand
Overall vs. Winners

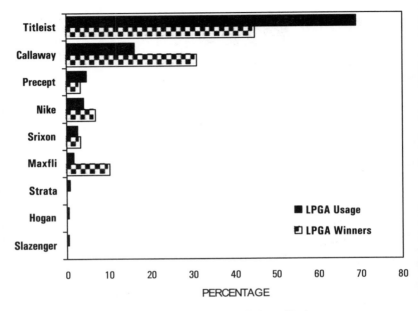

All 2003 LPGA Tournaments. Sample size: 3,827 players; 29 winners.
Every model used to win a tournament is on this chart.

While **Titleist** has by far the highest usage on the LPGA Tour, Callaway lays claim to nearly one in three wins.

Annika Sorenstam is a **Callaway** staff player. The sharp-eyed reader will be able to spot Annika's ball model on the opposite page.

Maxfli balls, fifth in usage, account for the third-highest number of LPGA wins.

LPGA Tour - Balls by Model

Overall vs. Winners

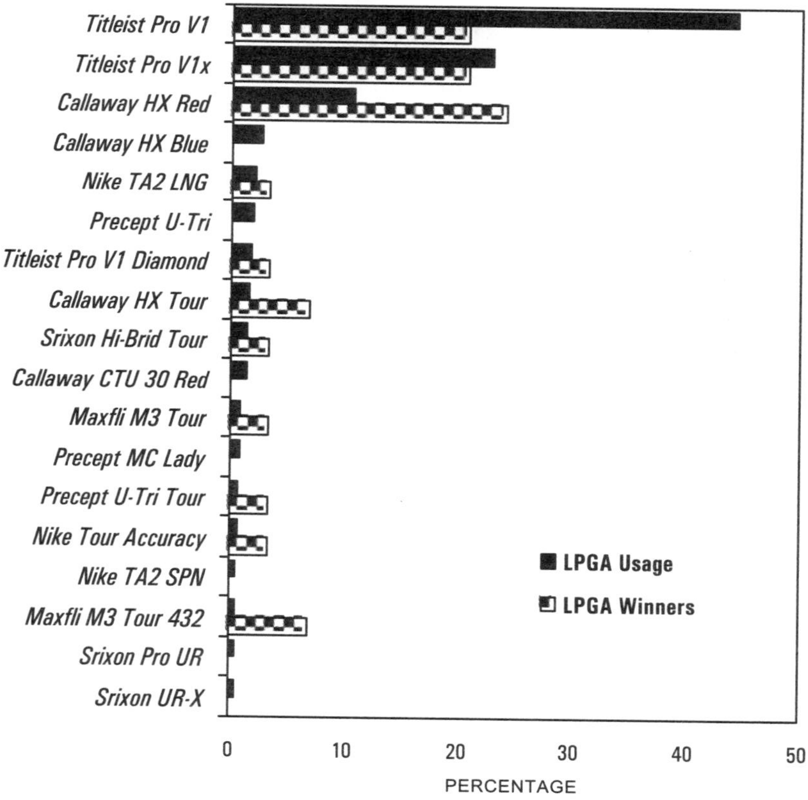

All 2003 LPGA Tournaments. Sample size: 3,857 players; 29 winners. Every model used to win a tournament is on this chart.

Titleist's **Pro V1** series accounts for the the two most popular models on the LPGA Tour in 2003, followed by Callaway's **HX series**.

Nike's **TA2 LNG** and **Tour Accuracy**, Srixon's **HiBrid Tour** and Maxfli's **M3 Tour Series** models also contribute to LPGAwins.

Japan Tour - Balls by Brand
Overall vs. Winners

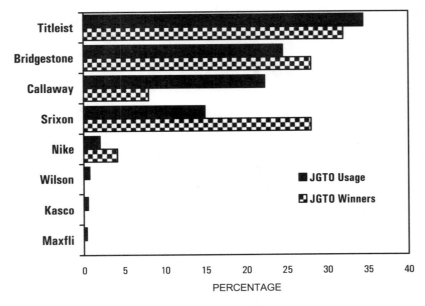

All 2003 JGTO Tournaments. Sample size: 3,342 players; 25 winners.
Every model used to win a tournament is on this chart.

Although **Titleist** balls lead in both **usage** and **victories** on the Japan Golf Tour in 2003, both **Bridgestone** and fourth-ranked **Srixon** rack up an impressive number of wins.

Third-place **Callaway** follows in wins.

Bridgestone and **Srixon** balls, less prevalent among U.S. pros, are a strong presence on the Japan Golf Tour.

Japan Tour - Balls by Model
Overall vs. Winners

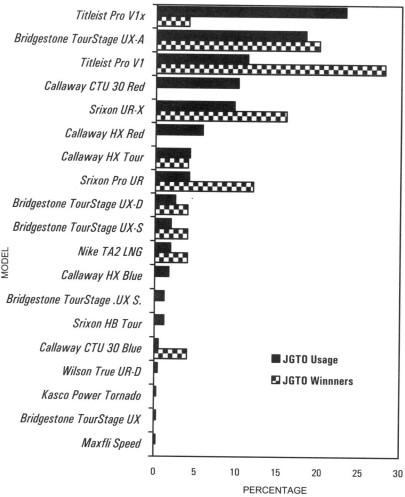

All 2003 JGTO Tournaments. Sample size: 3,342 players; 25 winners.
Every model used to win a tournament is on this chart.

Ten different ball models had wins on the JGTO in 2003.

The **Titleist Pro V1** and the **Bridgestone TourStage UX-A** are the models with the most victories.

Ball Statistics
2003 PGA Tour - Major Brands & Models

Ball Brand and Model	# of Uses	Sum of Official Money $	Average Winnings per Use $	Average Driving Accuracy %	Average Driving Distance Yards
BRIDGESTONE					
PRECEPT U-TRI TOUR	73	5,192,788.00	73,137.86	60.0	282.6
PRECEPT U-TRI	43	2,862,651.00	66,573.28	70.4	280.8
TOURSTAGE UX	52	1,661,535.00	33,230.70	61.0	280.7
TOURSTAGE UX-S	32	1,073,355.00	33,542.34	71.5	279.3
PREC. TOUR PREMIUM LS	45	901,774.00	20,494.86	60.2	278.8
PRECEPT U-TRI X-SPIN	9	750,817.00	83,424.11	57.8	287.4
TOURSTAGE UX-A	10	304,775.00	30,477.50	46.6	289.6
PRECEPT TOUR PREMIUM	2	162,000.00	81,000.00	53.6	287.1
TOURSTAGE U-DRIVE	3	36,755.00	12,251.67	73.6	288.8
Sum/Average of All Models	271	12,946,450.00	48,670.86	62.7	281.3
CALLAWAY					
CTU30 RED	364	8,883,134.00	25,236.18	61.8	283.4
HX TOUR	453	8,740,003.00	19,552.58	61.1	286.9
HX RED	294	5,776,731.00	20,127.98	57.6	283.2
CTU30 BLUE	17	136,734.00	8,043.18	57.0	282.4
HX BLUE	7	60,000.00	8,571.43	51.7	299.1
Sum/Average of All Models	1135	23,596,602.00	21,258.20	60.3	284.8
HOGAN					
APEX TOUR	243	6,502,105.00	27,435.04	62.6	280.9
APEX TOUR PLUS	7	209,385.00	29,912.14	53.8	283.5
Sum/Average of All Models	250	6,711,490.00	27,506.11	62.4	281.0
MAXFLI					
M3 TOUR 432	110	5,784,021.00	53,555.75	54.4	289.0
M3 TOUR	7	150,750.00	21,535.71	56.3	277.8
M3 TOUR 442	9	123,121.00	15,390.13	59.4	280.2
Sum/Average of All Models	133	6,057,892.00	46,599.17	53.8	286.9
NIKE					
T.ACCURACY II LONG	328	10,196,580.00	32,165.87	59.1	282.8
ONE TW	67	4,343,674.00	64,830.96	65.9	290.3
TOUR ACCURACY TW	9	3,287,250.00	410,906.25	61.6	287.5
T.ACCURACY II SPIN	157	2,062,473.00	13,306.28	60.2	282.1

Ball Statistics
2003 PGA Tour - Major Brands & Models

Ball Brand and Model	# of Uses	Sum of Official Money $	Average Winnings per Use $	Average Driving Accuracy %	Average Driving Distance Yards
NIKE (cont.)					
ONE	99	1,900,894.00	20,439.72	62.5	287.5
TOUR ACCURACY DD	9	57,893.00	6,432.56	31.6	275.9
TOUR ACCURACY	6	12,827.00	2,565.40	43.5	286.9
Sum/Average of All Models	680	21,861,591.00	33,173.89	59.9	284.2
SRIXON					
HI BRID TOUR	84	4,186,526.00	50,440.07	58.1	289.6
UR-X	40	1,126,762.00	28,891.33	57.4	283.4
PRO UR	20	284,023.00	14,201.15	63.3	277.5
HI BRID	2	30,000.00	15,000.00	50.0	286.3
Sum/Average of All Models	146	5,627,311.00	39,078.55	58.6	286.2
STRATA					
TOUR ACE	43	5,368,691.00	127,825.98	63.1	280.3
Sum/Average of All Models	43	5,368,691.00	127,825.98	63.1	280.3
TITLEIST					
PRO VI X	2374	94,965,524.00	41,181.93	59.0	289.0
PRO VI	1314	44,491,235.00	34,542.88	62.1	281.6
PRO VI STAR	62	2,463,176.00	39,728.65	59.1	282.1
PRO VI DIAMOND	20	834,910.00	41,745.50	61.0	269.1
Sum/Average of All Models	3770	142,754,845.00	38,834.29	60.1	286.2
WILSON					
TRUE TOUR ELITE	58	846,396.00	15,969.74	62.3	281.5
TRUE TOUR	16	104,197.00	6,946.47	47.9	282.3
Sum/Average of All Models	74	950,593.00	13,979.31	59.2	281.7

2003 Season, all PGA tournaments for which statistics are available. **Not all brands and**

2003 Season, all PGA tournaments for which statistics are available. Not all brands and models are listed above. Brand and overall sums and averages, however, do include all models and brands surveyed. 1 yard = 0.914 meters. $ = US Dollars. This data is copyrighted by Darrell Survey and may not be used without permission.

Money statistics are derived from PGA "official money" data; players failing to make the cut are averaged with zero earnings. Driving distance reflects the PGA "measured drives" statistic; driving accuracy is computed from the PGA "fairways hit" statistic. Cut players' driving distance and accuracy for rounds completed are included in the above averages.

Averages are less reliable for models with fewer than 50 uses.

IRONS

Chapter 2

IRONS: OVERVIEW AND TRENDS

The **diversity** of irons continues to increase in 2004, with pro golfers and consumers alike playing new or tried and true models from a wide range of clubmakers.

On the PGA Tour, **TaylorMade**, **Titleist** and **Cleveland** irons duke it out, with each brand scoring a significant share of usage overall and among the winning players *(see page 53)*. On the Champions and LPGA tours, **Callaway** and **Ping** are also top choices, while in Japan **Bridgestone** challenges TaylorMade for the top spot in irons. *(See pages 56, 60 & 62.)*

But, unlike with balls, the pros don't stick with only a few major companies when choosing their irons. Other brands with significant Tour usage in the U.S. and Japan include former PGA leader **Mizuno**, as well as **Nike, Hogan, Adams, MacGregor, Henry-Griffitts, Srixon, PRGR, Honma** and **Yonex**.

Among the wide variety of models favored by the pros are the TaylorMade 300 Forged, Cleveland TA1, Mizuno MP-33, Callaway Steelhead X-16 ProSeries, Nike Pro Combo, Hogan Apex, TaylorMade rac Forged, Ping i3+ and Titleist Forged 690 CB.

Nike Pro Combo
Cleveland Tour Action
Mizuno MP-33

On the **consumer** front, Callaway irons make a strong showing this year, with lower-handicaps choosing the Steelhead models and mid-handicaps selecting the Big Berthas. *(pages 40 - 41)*

The Ping i3+ and TaylorMade rac are popular new consumer irons, while Titleist's 690 MB and CB are chosen by the lowest-handicap consumers.

Just like the pros, however, **consumers are swinging with a vast array of iron brands**. Cleveland, Cobra, MacGregor, Nike and Nicklaus all show continuous growth in U.S. consumer iron usage over the past three years.

IRONS: OVERVIEW AND TRENDS

his year's ALMANAC features for the first time both *new* and *total* usage in reporting consumer club statistics. New usage, which is a brand or model's share of the equipment surveyed that was purchased in the past year, reflects the current marketplace. Total usage is a snapshot of all equipment currently in use, both new and old.

For categories that are slower to turn over, such as irons, **new and total consumer usage figures can diverge widely**. As seen on the chart on page 39, the venerable Ping Eye 2, introduced in 1982, still constitutes nearly 5% of the *total* iron sets in use across the U.S.A. In contrast, the Ping i3 is the top *new* model surveyed.

TaylorMade rac
Callaway X-16 Pro Series
Ping i3+

mong the iron models receiving the highest overall **Darrell Golfer Satisfaction Ratings** this year are the Mizuno MP-33 and T-Zoid, Cleveland TA5, Nike Pro Combo, TaylorMade 300 and Callaway Steelhead X-16 *(page 48& 49)*. Lower handicap consumers like Hogan Apex, while mid-handicaps give high marks to King Cobra irons *(page 40)*.

teel is the predominant **shaft material** for irons for pros and consumers alike. Only 22.9% of Nationwide Tour players use graphite-shafted irons; 26.3% of consumers do. **True Temper** and **Precision** are the top iron shafts on tour. Unlike the fast changing world of graphite shafts in pros' drivers, the most popular iron shaft models remain True Temper Dynamic Gold and Precision Rifle *(pages 64-65)*.

Similarly constant is the pros' preference for **Golf Pride iron grips.** In this year's analysis, we break out the cord and non-cord versions of such top models as the Tour Velvet and Victory, for your reference. *(See pages 66-67.)*

Consumer Irons Usage by Brand

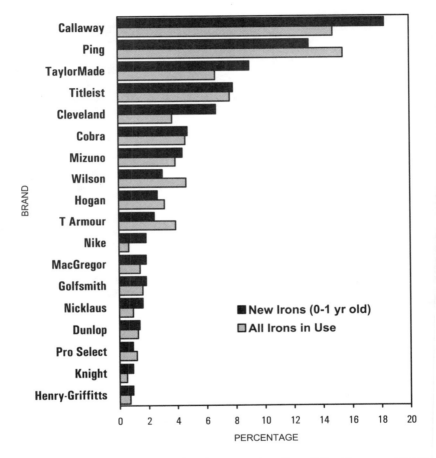

Percentage share of consumer equipment in use. Nationwide on-course consumer survey conducted summer 2003; 864 respondents for "New Irons" and 3,280 respondents for "Total Irons".

The Darrell Survey records the equipment recreational golfers actually use. Of the 864 golfers who bought new irons within the past year, more used Titleist irons than any other brand.

Of the total 3,280 golfers we interviewed in our 2003 national survey, more used Ping irons than any other brand.

Consumer Irons Usage by Model

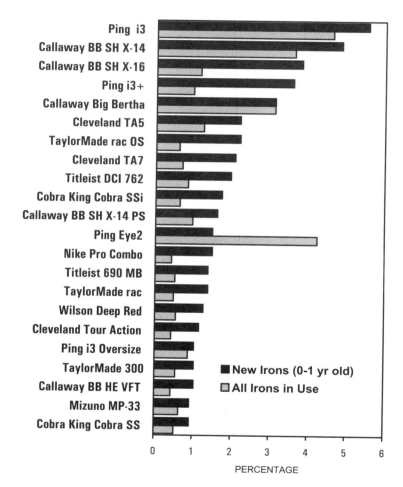

Percentage share of consumer equipment in use. Nationwide on-course consumer survey conducted summer 2003; 864 respondents for "New Irons" and 3,280 respondents for "Total Irons".

The table above reflects models used by recreational golfers in 2003.

Although comparatively fewer Ping Eye2 irons were bought within the last year (black), the clubs are still used by many golfers (gray).

Irons Model Usage by Handicap

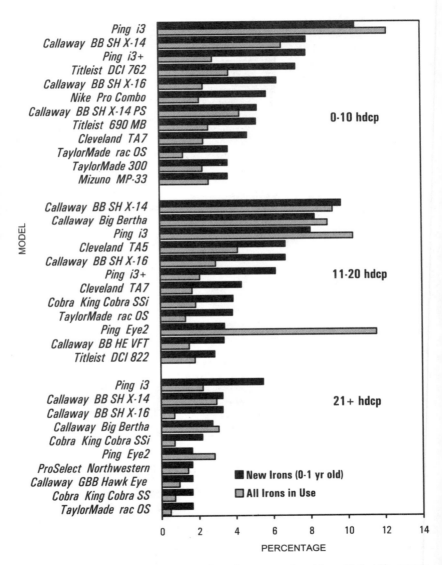

.Percentage share of consumer equipment in use. Nationwide on-course
consumer survey conducted summer 2003; 828 respondents for
"New Irons" and 3,171 respondents for "All Irons".

IRONS: WHAT CONSUMERS USE MOST

Irons Model Usage by Age

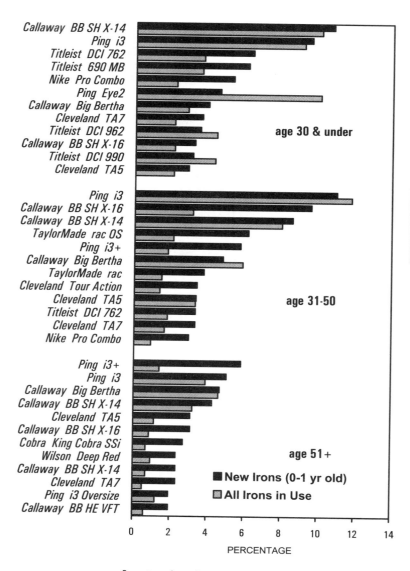

Percentage share of consumer equipment in use. Nationwide on-course consumer survey conducted summer 2003; 851 respondents for "New Irons" and 3,218 respondents for "All Irons".

What Set is Right for You?

(From top to Bottom) Titleust 762, Ping g2, RAM Tour Grind 802, Callaway Hawk Eye VFT, XPC 3000 & Yonex Cyberstar 3000

Consider Specialty Irons, Hybrid Woods

The popularity of hybrid clubs, designed to replace long irons in your bag, is changing the way golfers are thinking about sets. Now a hybrid club may read 2I/5W indicating a combination of a traditional iron and wood.

Popular models in this evolving area of clubmaking include such colorful names as Mizuno T-Zoid Fli Hi, TaylorMade Rescue, Cobra Baffler, Sonartec TD, Adams Idea, PRGR and the Fourteen Hi 850.

Some brands sell sets which involve hybrids like Adams' Idea .

Mizuno Hi Fli
Sonartec TD

There are many choices available now to the consumer. Instead of relying on a complete set, think about mixing it up.

Before standardized sets became the norm, clubs such as Cleeks, Baffies, Mashies and Niblicks were common. Could we be seeing a trend back to individual specialized clubs?

Probably not. The choices are confusing enough. But try out a few utility clubs and see what they can do for your game.

TaylorMade MId Fairway Rescue
Adams Idea (set)

Darrell Golfer Satisfaction Ratings™
Iron Brands by Handicap

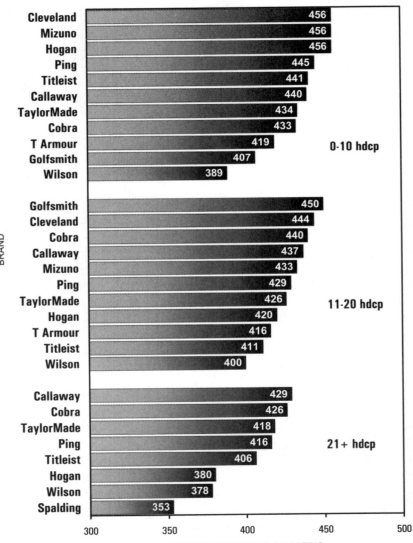

"How satisfied are you with your equipment?" 500 is most satisfied. 100 is least satisfied. Consumer golfers rate the equipment they are actually using the day of the survey. 2,267 opinion respondents. (Minimum of 15 responses per subgroup for brands shown.)

IRONS: CONSUMER OPINIONS

Darrell Golfer Satisfaction Ratings™
Iron Models by Handicap

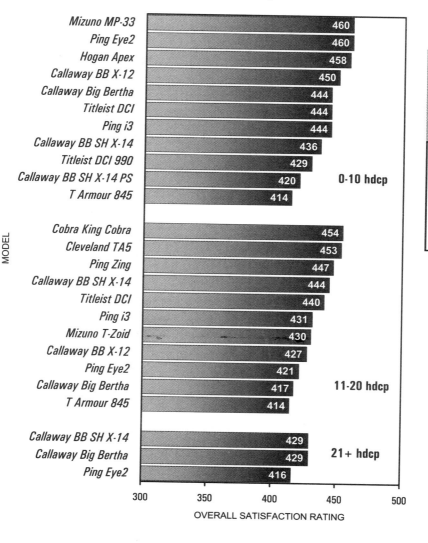

Irons

Consumer Opinions

"How satisfied are you with your equipment?" 500 is most satisfied. 100 is least satisfied.
Consumer golfers rate the equipment they are actually using the day of the survey. 2,267
opinion respondents. (Minimum of 12 responses per subgroup for models shown.)

Darrell Golfer Satisfaction Ratings™
Iron Brands by Age

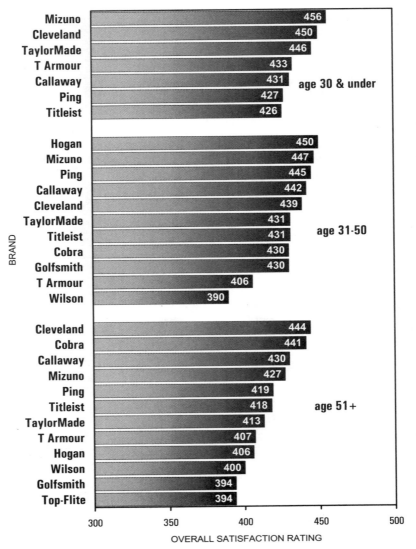

"How satisfied are you with your equipment?" 500 is most satisfied. 100 is least satisfied. Consumer golfers rate the equipment they are actually using the day of the survey. 2,267 opinion respondents. (Minimum of 15 responses per subgroup for brands shown.)

IRONS: CONSUMER OPINIONS

Darrell Golfer Satisfaction Ratings™
Iron Models by Age

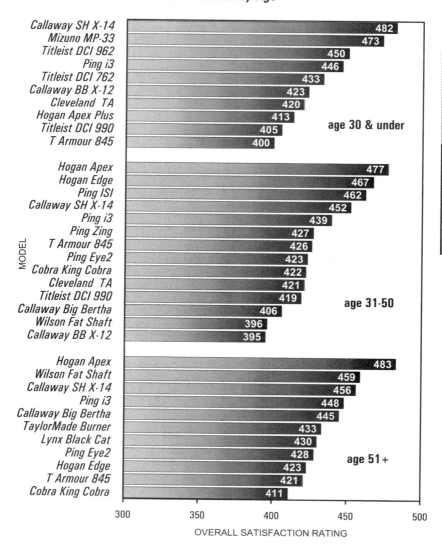

"How satisfied are you with your equipment?" 500 is most satisfied. 100 is least satisfied. Consumer golfers rate the equipment they are actually using the day of the survey. 2,267 opinion respondents. (Minimum of 10 responses per subgroup for models shown.)

Darrell Golfer Satisfaction Ratings™
Iron Brands by Feature

—— Satisfaction SCORE by Equipment Feature ——

IRONS

(Listed Alphabetically)	Overall	Value	Feel	Accuracy	Appearance	Forgiveness
Average Score	*418*	*421*	*420*	*420*	*415*	*410*
Callaway	*436*	*439*	426	434	*433*	*439*
Cleveland	*442*	*445*	*431*	*441*	*432*	*424*
Cobra	*435*	*436*	*437*	*439*	426	*432*
Dunlop	348	344	381	352	344	341
Golfsmith	412	414	426	421	412	400
Hogan	426	431	423	434	426	412
Lynx	390	395	395	390	386	385
MacGregor	381	389	379	404	375	371
Mizuno	*446*	*450*	*433*	*452*	*439*	421
Nicklaus	389	400	379	400	400	389
Nike	*450*	*450*	425	*462*	*450*	394
Ping	433	*438*	*433*	430	*435*	*431*
Pro Select	333	333	390	320	329	305
Ram	412	412	*431*	387	406	407
Spalding	381	373	396	377	364	365
T Armour	414	418	423	411	416	400
TaylorMade	427	431	423	*437*	420	*422*
Titleist	425	428	421	433	426	·410
Top-Flite	400	388	400	385	391	382
Wilson	390	398	411	395	390	382

"How satisfied are you with your equipment?" 500 is most satisfied. 100 is least satisfied. Consumer golfers rate the equipment they are actually using the day of the survey. 2,267 opinion respondents. (Minimum of 15 responses per subgroup for brands shown.)

❖ Compare each score to the average seen in the top row.
❖ Numbers in *bold italic* indicate top 5 scores in each category.
❖ Scores for individual models are listed on the opposite page.

The **Nike, Mizuno, Cleveland, Callaway** and **Cobra** iron brands received the highest overall satisfaction ratings in our nationwide survey.

Nike's Pro Combo, Callaway's Steelhead X-16, TaylorMade's 300 and Titleist's DCI 762 models receive high satisfaction ratings in accuracy. *(See opposite page.)*

Darrell Golfer Satisfaction Ratings™
Iron Models by Feature

—— Satisfaction SCORE by Equipment Feature ——

IRONS (Listed Alphabetically)	Overall	Value	Feel	Accuracy	Appearance	Forgiveness
Average Score	418	421	420	420	415	410
Callaway BB X-12	433	431	420	425	435	438
Callaway BB SH X-14	437	441	429	435	430	434
Callaway BB SH X-14 PS	428	428	422	428	433	*444*
Callaway BB SH X-16	447	*461*	428	*461*	*450*	*450*
Callaway Big Bertha	431	444	422	426	429	*440*
Cleveland TA5	448	*456*	441	444	444	437
Cleveland Tour Action	*450*	451	*450*	446	439	429
Cobra King Cobra	435	437	441	441	430	437
Cobra King Cobra II	425	431	437	425	400	412
Cobra Lady	*450*	444	*444*	450	*450*	*450*
Hogan Apex	434	439	426	443	434	423
Hogan Apex Edge	430	425	420	430	425	420
Mizuno MP	*451*	*457*	426	459	*452*	429
Mizuno MP-33	*460*	*469*	*446*	456	*465*	*448*
Mizuno T-Zoid	449	455	**440**	*457*	442	422
Nicklaus	389	400	379	400	400	389
Nike Pro Combo	*450*	450	425	*462*	*450*	394
Ping Eye2	427	432	438	416	432	429
Ping i3	436	446	432	445	440	431
Ping ISI	394	400	394	388	400	382
Ping Zing	443	443	*446*	430	446	435
T Armour 845	411	419	425	411	417	398
TaylorMade 300	*450*	*469*	*444*	*462*	*462*	431
TaylorMade 320	428	428	406	450	422	422
TaylorMade rac	426	432	426	442	416	421
Titleist DCI 762	440	455	435	*460*	435	420
Titleist DCI 981	414	414	423	409	414	405
Titleist DCI 990	417	417	407	423	420	397
Wilson Fat Shaft	411	421	424	411	405	413
Wilson Staff	396	400	423	400	396	387

Irons

Consumer Opinions

"How satisfied are you with your equipment?" 500 is most satisfied. 100 is least satisfied. Numbers in **bold italic** indicate top 5 scores for each category. Consumer golfers rate the equipment they are actually using the day of the survey. 2,267 opinion respondents. (Minimum of 12 responses per subgroup for models shown.)

Breaking the Mold

The variety of **forged irons** from golf club manufacturers is staggering. Hogan and Nike offer forged irons only, and forgings from companies such as Titleist, TaylorMade, MacGregor, Cobra and Orlimar have made a huge impact in golf. Even Callaway, which sells cast irons, introduced forged wedges.

Many of the most popular iron sets—including all Pings, Callaways and the DCI from Titleist—are **cast**. Annika Sorenstam, who pound-for-pound may be the best golfer in the world, uses cast Callaways.

Whether cast or forged, irons today offer a **tremendous value**. In fact, all golf club prices have come down in recent years and represent a bargain in today's marketplace.

Golfers probably would be well-advised to pay as much attention to the **shaft** as the clubhead in irons. The shaft choice is between steel and graphite, and it is a fascinating tug-of-war.

For older players, most women and those with **slower swing speeds**, **graphite** offers several inherent advantages. Graphite has wonderful shock absorption capabilities. It also weighs less than steel, allowing more weight to be placed in the clubhead. (See *pages 64 & 66* to review the iron shafts chosen by touring professionals.)

With irons, the cardinal rule of consumerism should be followed once again: **Try out** a variety of clubs before making a purchase decision.

And don't assume that the iron models used by the top touring professionals in the world will necessarily be the best choice for you.

Hogan Apex Edge
Tiltleist 690 CB
Cobra Forged SS

Top Irons Models
At Major Amateur Events

U.S. AMATEUR
Ping Blade i3
Mizuno MP-33
Callaway Steelhead X-14 PS
Titleist DCI 990
TaylorMade 300
Titleist 690 MB
Mizuno MP-14
Titleist DCI 962
Hogan Apex
Ping Eye 2
Ping i3 O-Size

U.S. WOMEN'S AMATEUR
Callaway Steelhead X-14
Callaway Big Bertha X-12
Ping i3
Callaway Steelhead X-14 PS
Ping i3 O-Size
Titleist DCI 981
Titleist DCI 962
Ping ISI
Titleist DCI 762

NCAA DIV. 1 MEN'S
Ping Blade i3
Titleist DCI 990
Mizuno MP-33
TaylorMade 300
Cleveland TA1
Callaway Steelhead X-14 PS
Cleveland TA 3
Ping i3 O-Size
Titleist 690.MB

NCAA WOMEN'S
Callaway Steelhead X-14
Callaway Steelhead X-14 PS
Ping i3 O-Size
Ping Blade i3
Callaway Big Bertha X-12
Titleist DCI 981
Callaway Big Bertha X-12 PS
Titleist DCI 762

U.S. BOYS JUNIOR
Mizuno MP-33
Titleist DCI 990
Callaway Steelhead X-14 PS
Ping Blade i3
Titleist 690.MB
Titleist DCI 962
Cleveland TA 3
TaylorMade 300
Mizuno T-Zoid Pro2
Titleist DCI 762

U.S. GIRLS JUNIOR
Callaway Steelhead X-14
Ping i3 O-Size
Ping Blade i3
Titleist DCI 981
Callaway Big Bertha X-12
Titleist DCI 762
Titleist DCI 981SL
Ping ISI
Callaway Hawk Eye
Henry-Griffitts
Titleist DCI 990

2003 Data. Listed in order of decreasing usage at each tournament.

This page shows the wide array of iron models used by top players at the competitive amateur level. A young, gifted player would be would be well served to play with any of these sets.

Irons

Amateur Usage

Matched Iron Sets on Tour

W hat is the most common iron set used by the pros? The chart below shows some stark differences. Nearly 60% of the **PGA Tour** golfers use a **3-9 set**, while only 15% of **LPGA** golfers do.

Many good players have a 1- or 2-iron that does not match their set.

Champions Tour players go for a 3-9 or **4-9 set**, while the ladies prefer to keep more room in the bag for extra fairway woods by using fewer iron clubs (*see page 123 for more on fairway woods*).

	Matched Iron Set Used on Tour					
	1-9	**2-9**	**3-9**	**4-9**	**5-9**	**6-9**
	%	%	%	%	%	%
PGA	0.02	17.9	59.8	12.1	5.9	1.4
Champions	0.04	8.4	50.2	32.4	4.3	1.7
LPGA	0.00	1.0	14.7	49.8	27.5	6.3

2003 season. All tournaments surveyed. Some 5-9 & 6-9 sets are part of a split set.

B ut the story doesn't end with the traditional iron set. One-third of PGA tournament players **tinker with their iron sets** in some way — by picking and choosing among different iron models, by skipping the 2 or 3 iron, by using specialty (utility) long irons, or by any combination of the above.

More than one quarter of Champions Tour players customize their iron sets. But less than one in ten of LPGA golfers do so.

Customized sets*	
	%
PGA	33.9
Champions	27.1
LPGA	8.6

2003 season

*Percentage of players with more than a standard set of irons: different models mixed in, long irons, utility irons, skipped clubs, etc.

Tour - Irons by Brand

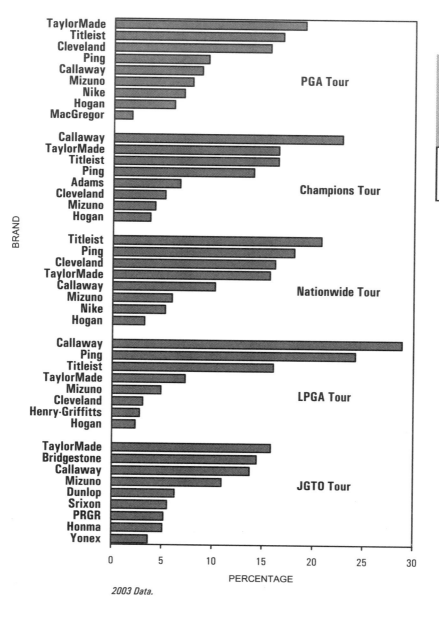

2003 Data.

PGA Tour - Irons by Brand
Overall vs. Winners

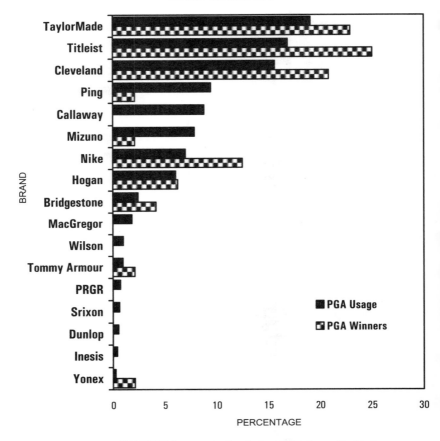

All 2003 PGA Tournaments. Sample size: : 6,507 players; 48 winners.

*All other iron brands used on PGA Tour in 2003: **Adams, Cobra, Founders Club, Golfsmith, Guerin Rife, Henry-Griffitts, Infiniti, M Golf, Maruman, Maxfli, Nicklaus, Vulcan.***

TaylorMade leads the PGA Tour in irons usage, but **Titleist** has the edge in victories. **Cleveland** takes third place in both irons usage and wins.

Using the list of PGA tournament winners on page 207, you can deduce that the Yonex win came from Scott Hoch.

IRONS: PRO USAGE

PGA Tour - Irons by Model
Overall vs. Winners

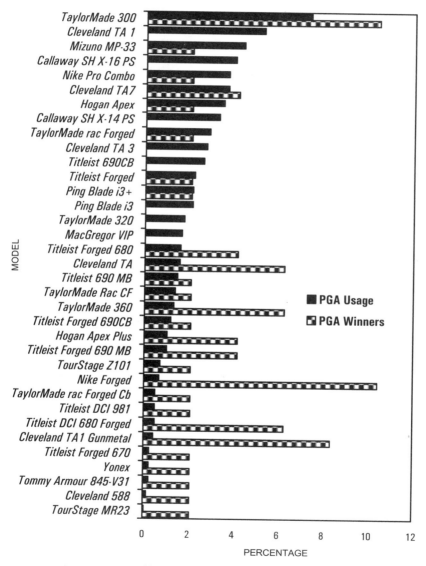

All 2003 PGA Tournaments. Sample size: 6,507 players; 48 winners.
Every model used to win a tournament is on this chart.

Champions Tour - Irons by Brand
Overall vs. Winners

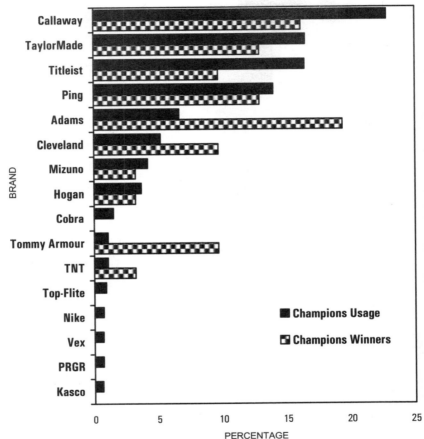

All 2003 Champions Tournaments. Sample size: 2,604 players; 31 winners.

*Every brand used to win a tournament is on this chart. All other iron brands used on Champions Tour in 2003: **Bullet, Chicago, Dean Ota, Founders Club, Henry-Griffitts, Honma, J Riley, Lynx, Maxfli, Nicklaus, Orlimar, Pax, Power Arc, Powerbilt, Precept, Pure Spin, Slazenger, Srixon, Tour Edge, Wilson, Yonex.***

Callaway irons lead in overall usage on the Champions Tour, while **Adams** leads in winners.

Ten different brands of irons contributed to 31 wins on the 2003 Champions Tour. *See pages 208-209 for a list of tournament winners.*

Champions Tour - Irons by Model
Overall vs. Winners

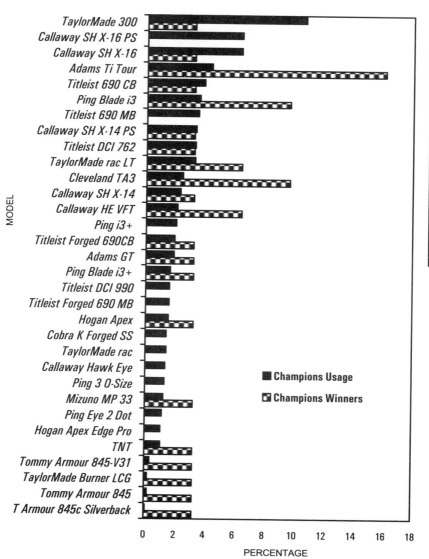

Irons

Tour

Champions

All 2003 Champions Tournaments. Sample size: 2,604 players; 31 winners. Every model used to win a tournament is on this chart.

Nationwide Tour - Irons by Brand
Overall vs. Winners

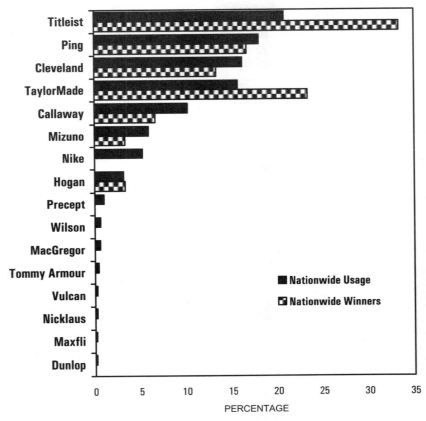

All 2003 Nationwide Tournaments. Sample size: 2,604 players; 31 winners.

Every brand used to win a tournament is on this chart. All other iron brands used on Nationwide Tour in 2003: Bullet, Chicago, Dean Ota, Founders Club, Henry-Griffitts, Honma, J Riley, Lynx, Maxfli, Nicklaus, Orlimar, Pax, Power Arc, Powerbilt, Precept, Pure Spin, Slazenger, Srixon, Tour Edge, Wilson, Yonex.

On the Nationwide Tour, **Titleist** irons lead in both usage and wins.

As seen on the opposite page, while the **Ping i3+ Blade** is the most used model, several models tie for the greatest number of wins: Titleist's 690.CB & DCI 990, Ping's Zing 2 and the TaylorMade 360.

Nationwide Tour - Irons by Brand
Overall vs. Winners

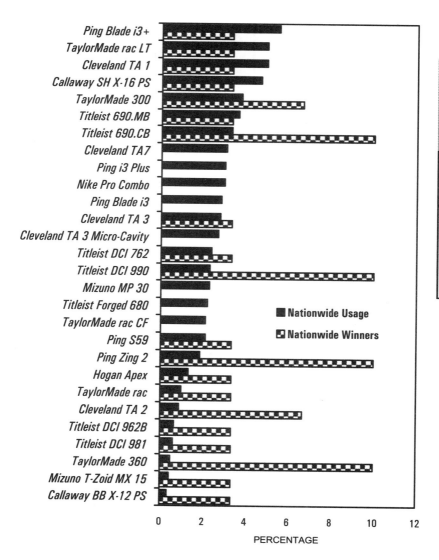

All 2003 Nationwide Tournaments. Sample size: 4,476 players; 30 winners. Every model used to win a tournament is on this chart.

Irons

Tour

Nationwide

LPGA Tour - Irons by Brand
Overall vs. Winners

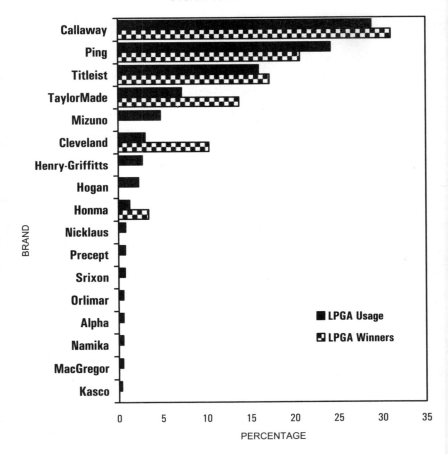

All 2003 LPGA Tournaments. Sample size: 3,857 players; 29 winners. Every brand used to win a tournament is on this chart. All other iron brands used on LPGA Tour in 2003: *Acura, Cobra, E Lord, Infiniti, Jazz, KZG, Lopez, M Golf, Makser, Maxfli, Meridian, Montech, Nike, Onoff, Pax, Razor, S Yard, Wilson, Yonex.*

Callaway leads the LPGA in irons, with spirited competition from **Ping, Titleist** and **TaylorMade.**

Thirteen different models contributed to victories *(see opposite page).*

LPGA Tour - Irons by Model
Overall vs. Winners

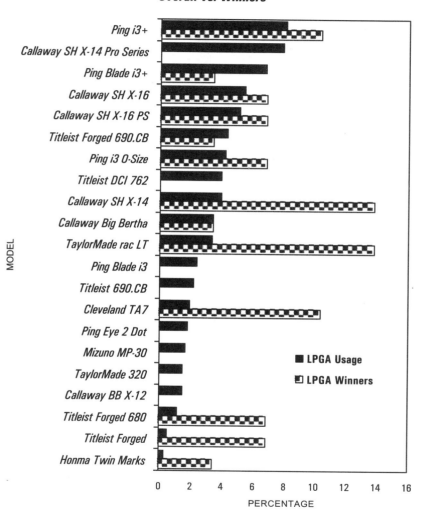

All 2003 LPGA Tournaments. Sample size: 3,857 players; 29 winners.
Every model used to win a tournament is on this chart.

Although the **Ping i3+** model is the most popular on the LPGA Tour in 2003, **Callaway Steelhead X-14** and **TaylorMade rac ST** tie for the greatest number of wins.

Japan Tour - Irons by Brand
Overall vs. Winners

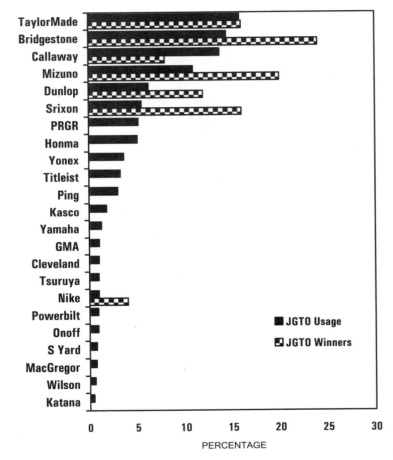

All 2003 JGTO Tournaments. Sample size: 3,366 players; 25 winners.
Every brand used to win a tournament is on this chart. All other iron brands
used on JGTO Tour in 2003: **Crews, Daiwa, Fourteen, Grand Prix,**
H. Matsumoto, Hogan, Joy Many, Kamui, Maruman, Miura, Royal
Collection, Tour Concept, Vex.

Although **TaylorMade** leads the irons count on the Japan Golf Tour in 2003, Bridgestone chalks up the most wins.

Sixteen different iron models scored wins on the Japan Tour in 2003.

Japan Tour - Irons by Model
Overall vs. Winners

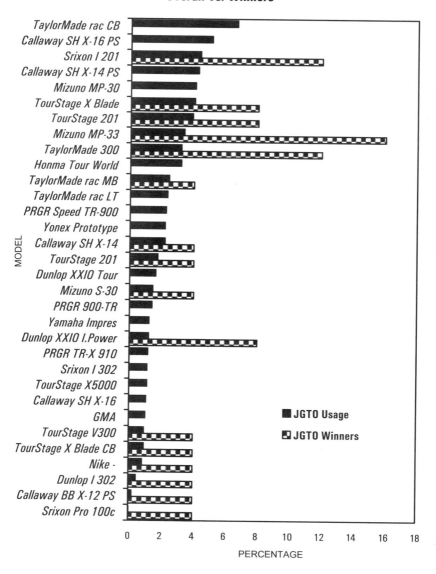

All 2003 JGTO Tournaments. Sample size: 3,366 players; 25 winners.
Every model used to win a tournament is on this chart.

Tour - Irons Shafts by Brand
(Graphite & Steel)

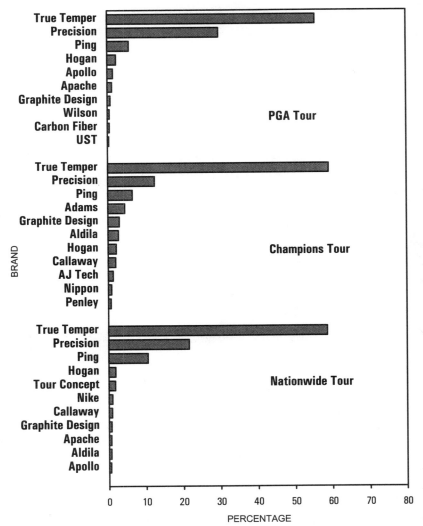

Descending order of leading model usage for each tour, 2003 data.
Selected events.

Nearly all irons on the men's U.S. tours have **True Temper** or **Precision** brand shafts.

Tour - Irons Shafts by Model
(Graphite & Steel)

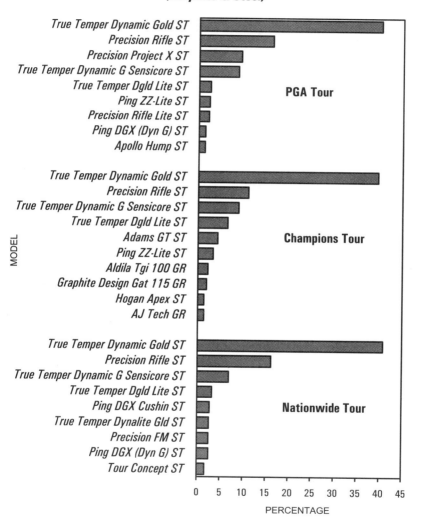

Descending order of leading model usage for each tour, 2003 data. Selected events.

The leading iron-shaft models on the major U.S. men's tours are **steel**, in a stark contrast to the prevalence of **graphite** in driver shafts *(see page 115).*

Tour - Irons Grips by Brand

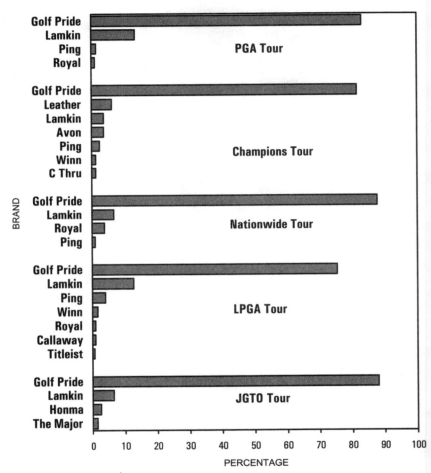

Descending order of leading brand usage for each tour. Leather grips are not surveyed by brand. 2003 data, selected events.

Golf Pride is far and away the leading supplier of grips for irons on the major tours in the U.S. and Japan.

It is interesting to compare the models of grips used for irons to those for drivers *(pages 116-117)* and putters *(pages 182-183)*.

Tour - Irons Grips by Model

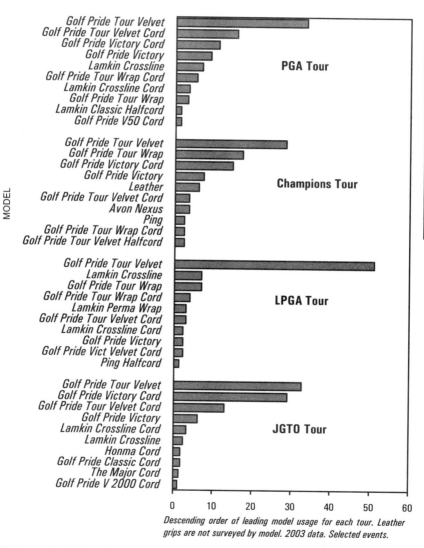

MODEL

Golf Pride Tour Velvet
Golf Pride Tour Velvet Cord
Golf Pride Victory Cord
Golf Pride Victory
Lamkin Crossline
Golf Pride Tour Wrap Cord
Lamkin Crossline Cord
Golf Pride Tour Wrap
Lamkin Classic Halfcord
Golf Pride V50 Cord

PGA Tour

Golf Pride Tour Velvet
Golf Pride Tour Wrap
Golf Pride Victory Cord
Golf Pride Victory
Leather
Golf Pride Tour Velvet Cord
Avon Nexus
Ping
Golf Pride Tour Wrap Cord
Golf Pride Tour Velvet Halfcord

Champions Tour

Golf Pride Tour Velvet
Lamkin Crossline
Golf Pride Tour Wrap
Golf Pride Tour Wrap Cord
Lamkin Perma Wrap
Golf Pride Tour Velvet Cord
Lamkin Crossline Cord
Golf Pride Victory
Golf Pride Vict Velvet Cord
Ping Halfcord

LPGA Tour

Golf Pride Tour Velvet
Golf Pride Victory Cord
Golf Pride Tour Velvet Cord
Golf Pride Victory
Lamkin Crossline Cord
Lamkin Crossline
Honma Cord
Golf Pride Classic Cord
The Major Cord
Golf Pride V 2000 Cord

JGTO Tour

0   10   20   30   40   50   60

Descending order of leading model usage for each tour. Leather grips are not surveyed by model. 2003 data. Selected events.

Irons

Tour

Grips

This analysis breaks down each grip model into its cord and non-cord versions. PGA players like the **Tour Velvet** best—cord or not.

WEDGES

Chapter 3

The Way of the Wedge

Wedges are a hot topic. Now widely recognized as a vital part of a golfer's arsenal, wedges are available in greater variety and finer quality than ever before.

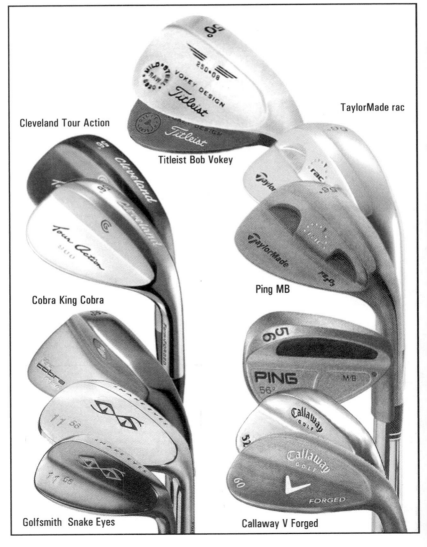

TaylorMade rac

Cleveland Tour Action

Titleist Bob Vokey

Cobra King Cobra

Ping MB

Golfsmith Snake Eyes

Callaway V Forged

Darrell Golfer Satisfaction Ratings™
Pitching Wedge Brands by Handicap

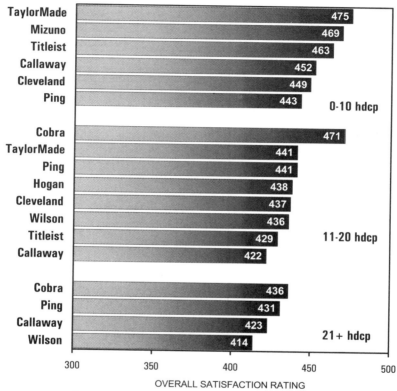

OVERALL SATISFACTION RATING

"How satisfied are you with your equipment?" 500 is most satisfied. 100 is least satisfied. Consumer golfers rate the equipment they are actually using the day of the survey. 2,253 opinion respondents. (Minimum of 15 responses per subgroup for brands shown.)

Newly added to this year's ALMANAC are Wedge Satisfaction Ratings, taken from our survey of more than 2,000 consumer golfers across the U.S.A.

While low-handicap golfers rate their TaylorMade pitching wedges the highest, among higher-handicap golfers, Cobra is the most favored brand.

Pitching wedges are typically purchased as part of an iron set. Compare this page with ratings of irons *(see page 76.)*

Darrell Golfer Satisfaction Ratings™
Lob, Sand, Gap Wedge Brands by Handicap

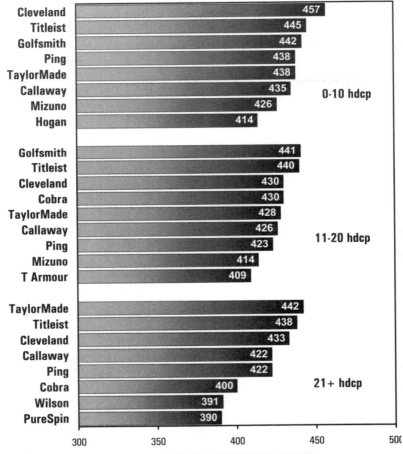

Brand	Rating	Group
Cleveland	457	0-10 hdcp
Titleist	445	
Golfsmith	442	
Ping	438	
TaylorMade	438	
Callaway	435	
Mizuno	426	
Hogan	414	
Golfsmith	441	11-20 hdcp
Titleist	440	
Cleveland	430	
Cobra	430	
TaylorMade	428	
Callaway	426	
Ping	423	
Mizuno	414	
T Armour	409	
TaylorMade	442	21+ hdcp
Titleist	438	
Cleveland	433	
Callaway	422	
Ping	422	
Cobra	400	
Wilson	391	
PureSpin	390	

OVERALL SATISFACTION RATING

"How satisfied are you with your equipment?" 500 is most satisfied. 100 is least satisfied. Consumer golfers rate the equipment they are actually using the day of the survey. 2,253 opinion respondents. (Minimum of 15 responses per subgroup for brands shown.)

These facing pages **omit pitching wedges**. Sand, gap and lob wedges are often treated as individual club purchases by better golfers.

Low-handicap consumers rate Cleveland non-pitching wedges highest overall, with a satisfaction score of 457 out of a perfect 500.

WEDGES: CONSUMER OPINIONS

Darrell Golfer Satisfaction Ratings™
Lob, Sand, Gap Wedge Models by Handicap

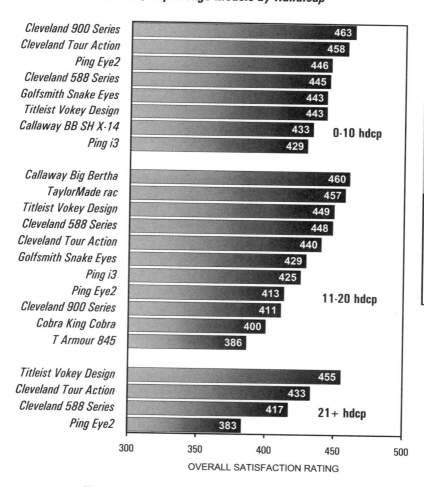

"How satisfied are you with your equipment?" 500 is most satisfied. 100 is least satisfied. Consumer golfers rate the equipment they are actually using the day of the survey.
2,253 opinion respondents. (Minimum of 12 responses per subgroup for models shown.)

In this handicap-specific analysis of non-pitching wedges, Cleveland,
Ping, Callaway, TaylorMade and Titleist all have high-scoring wedge
models.

Tour - All Wedges by Brand

Long-time PGA Tour leader **Cleveland** ekes out a win this year for total wedges in play, but **Titleist** wedges win out among Champions and LPGA players *(see page 75)*. **TaylorMade** leads in total wedges on the Japan Golf Tour.

Among the pros' favorite models are the Cleveland 588 and 900, Titleist Bob Vokey, Ping MB, Adams Tom Watson, TaylorMade rac and Callaway V Forged.

The models of pitching wedges, as seen on page 79, are quite different from the models of sand, gap and lob wedges. Pitching wedge models resemble the variety of irons models. Cleveland and Titleist are the most popular brands of sand, gap and lob wedges *(see page 82.)*

Bounce is one of the most crucial features of any wedge, particularly a sand wedge. The bounce **angle** of the sole helps determine how much a sand wedge will bounce (or, conversely, how much it will dig in) on a sand shot. Most golfers need a considerable amount of bounce on their sand wedges in order to be effective in greenside bunkers.

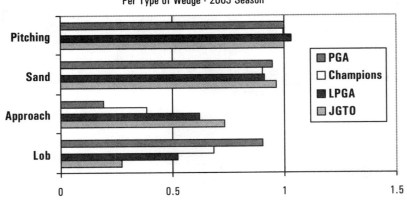

Average Number of Wedges Used by Tour Players
Per Type of Wedge - 2003 Season

WEDGES: PRO USAGE

Tour - All Wedges by Brand

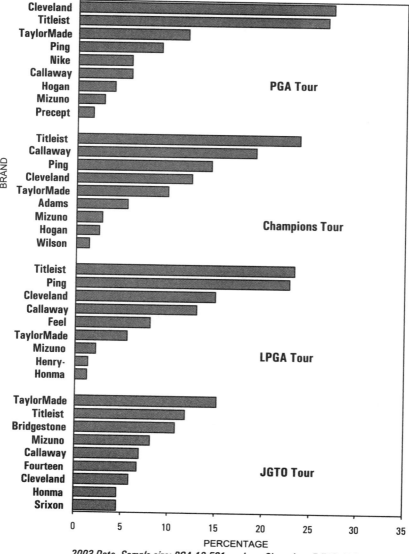

2003 Data. Sample size: PGA 13,591 wedges; Champions 7,713; LPGA 11,899; LGTO 9,912. Descending order of usage per tour.

Tour - Pitching Wedges by Brand

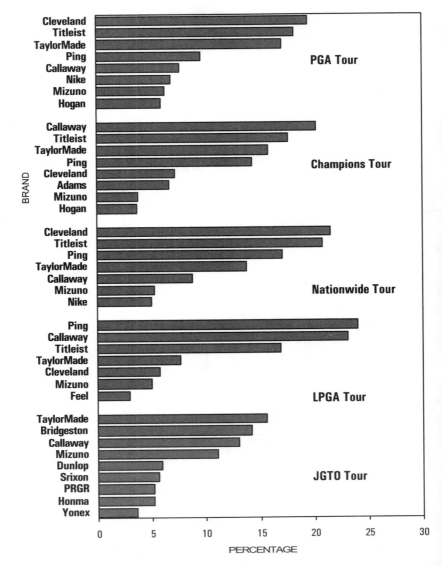

2003 Data. Sample size: PGA 6,505 wedges; Champions 2,587; Nationwide 4,509; LPGA 3,977; LGTO 3,339. Descending order of usage per tour.

WEDGES: PRO USAGE

Tour - Pitching Wedges by Model

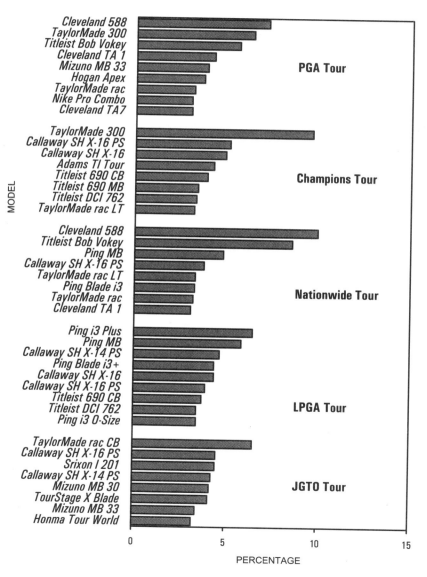

2003 Data. Sample size: PGA 6,505 wedges; Champions 2,587; Nationwide 4,509; LPGA 3,977; JGTO 3,339. Descending order of usage per tour.

WEDGES: PRO USAGE

Tour - Sand Wedges by Brand

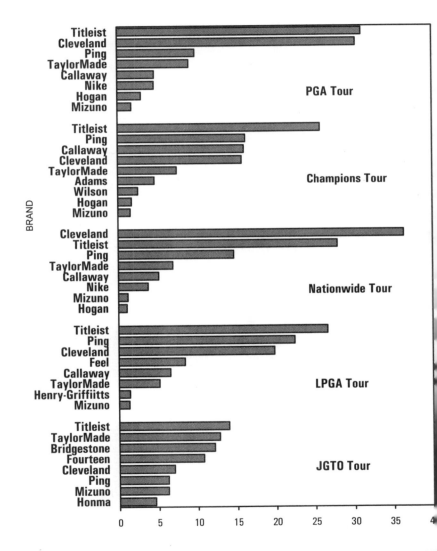

2003 Data. Sample size: PGA 6,166 wedges; Champions 2,351; Nationwide 4,315; LPGA 3,518; JTGO 3,321. Descending order of usage per tour.

Cleveland sand wedges are especially popular on the Nationwide Tour, while Titleist is the leading sand wedge on the other tours.

WEDGES: PRO USAGE

Tour - Sand Wedges by Model

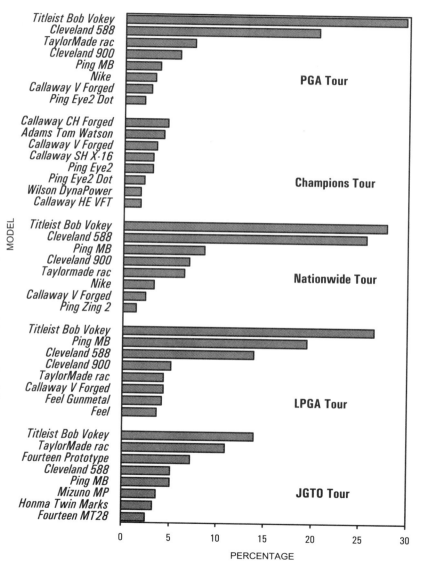

2003 Data. Sample size: PGA 6,166 wedges; Champions 2,351; Nationwide
4,315; LPGA 3,518; JGTO 3,221. Descending order of usage per tour.

Tour - Lob Wedges by Brand

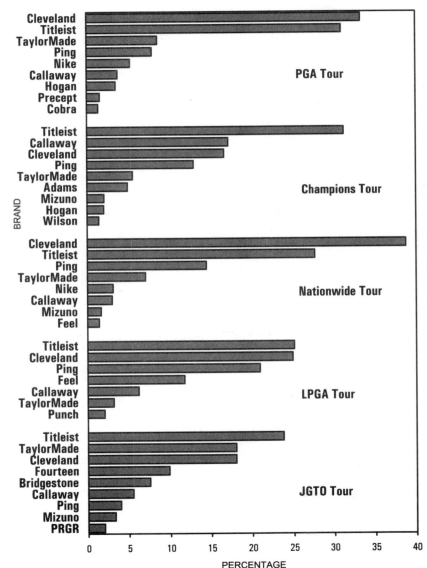

PERCENTAGE

2003 Data. Sample size: PGA 5,858 wedges; Champions 1,781; Nationwide 4,054; LPGA 2,012; JGTO 904. Descending order of usage per tour.

WEDGES: PRO USAGE

Tour - Lob Wedges by Model

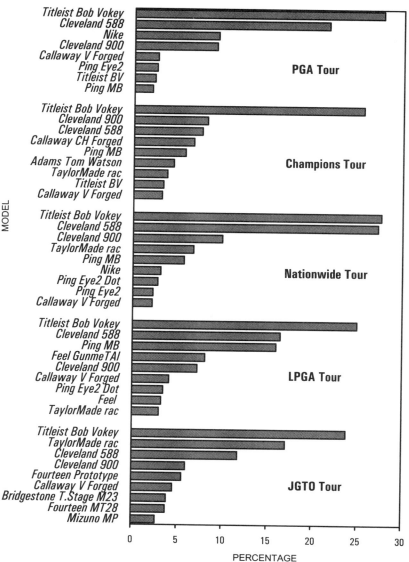

2003 Data. Sample size: PGA 5,0558 wedges; Champions 1,781; Nationwide 4,054; LPGA 2,088; JGTO 904. Descending order of usage per tour.

Tour - Sand/Gap/Lob Wedges by Brand

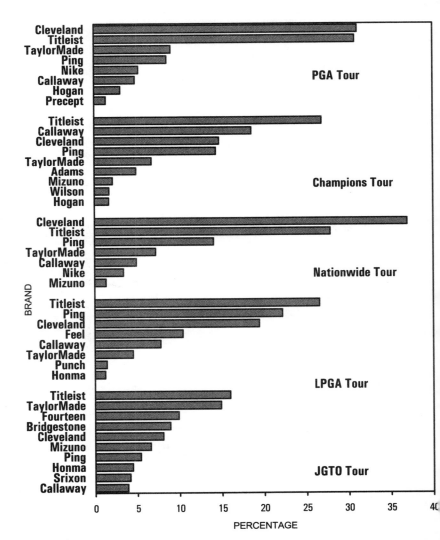

2003 Data. Sample size: PGA 13,259 wedges; Champions 5,132; Nationwide 9,082; LPGA 7,922; JGTO 6,573. Descending order of usage per tour.

Since pitching wedges closely correlate to irons, it is interesting to **remove** them from the equation for one final analsyis.

DRIVERS

Chapter 4

DRIVERS: OVERVIEW

This year we saw a **more diverse** range of drivers than we have since the downfall of the wood-headed wood in the 1980s. After metalwood innovator **TaylorMade** dominated drivers, then **Callaway** took over. Now, many different brands and models capture the attention of pros and consumers alike.

Five years ago, Callaway and TaylorMade accounted for more than half of the new consumer drivers in use. Today, this year's top two consumer drivers, TaylorMade and **Titleist**, make up only one third of new equipment usage *(see page 86).*

TaylorMade R510 TP

Among pros, TaylorMade drivers are number one on the PGA and Nationwide Tours, while Callaway takes top honors on the LPGA. The battle on the Champions and Japan Golf Tours is so **fierce** that Callaway and TaylorMade drivers virtually tie, although TaylorMade has the edge in wins *(see pages 103-113).*

But the brands at the top of the count aren't the only story this year. Titleist, **Nike**, **Cleveland**, **Ping**, **Adams**, **Bridgestone**, **Srixon** and **Mizuno** drivers are also major players on one or more tours.

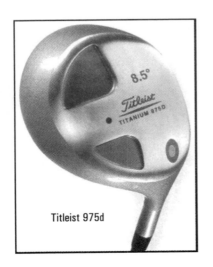

Titleist 975d

Among the top driver models in pro usage this season are the TaylorMade R510 and R580, Titleist 983k and 983e, Callaway GBB II & GBB II ProSeries), Adams Redline Tour, Ping Si3, Cleveland Launcher and the Japanese Bridgestone X-Drive 300.

Driver models with the **longest average PGA driving distances** include the Callaway ERC Fusion, Cleveland Launcher 400 and the MacGregor V Foil *(see page 97).*

DRIVERS: OVERVIEW

While TaylorMade and Titleist successfully retained their **consumer** driver customers this year, Callaway and Ping saw some of their players move to the such brands as Cobra and Cleveland for their new drivers*(see pages 86 to 89)*.

Among the most widely used new consumer drivers are the TaylorMade R580, Titleist 983K, Callaway Great Big Bertha II and the King Cobra SS 427 *(page 87-89)*.

Cobra drivers come on strong in **driver satisfaction ratings**, with several of the King Cobra models ranked highly in our nationwide consumer survey. The Cleveland Launcher 400 and Callaway Great Big Bertha II also garner top overall satisfaction honors. *(page 97)*

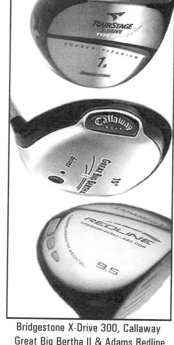

Bridgestone X-Drive 300, Callaway Great Big Bertha II & Adams Redline

Golf Pride Grips

Driver shafts are a very competitive category in and of themselves on the pro tours, with **Fujikura, Grafalloy, Graphite Design** among the leading brands. The Fujikura Six, Graphite Design YS6, Grafalloy Blue are among the pros' top choices *(see pages 114 & 115 for shaft data)*.

For their **driver grips**, the pros prefer the Golf Pride brand. In this year's ALMANAC, we break out the grip models by cord and non-cord designs. Thus we see that the G.P. Tour Velvet is tops on the U.S. tours, while Japan Golf Tour players like G.P. Victory Cord best *(see pages 116 & 117)*.

Drivers

Overview

Consumer Driver Usage by Brand

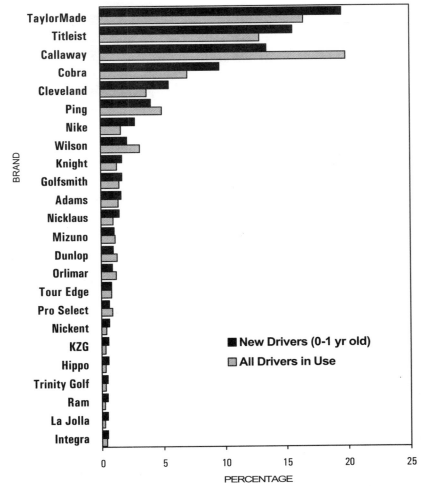

Black bars show brand share of new (less than 1 year old) equipment in use. Gray bars show percentage of all consumer equipment in use. Nationwide on-course consumer survey conducted summer 2003; 3,151 respondents.

Among golfers who acquired their driver within the past year, more chose **TaylorMade** than any other brand.

But among *all* drivers observed in 2003, new and old, more players chose **Callaway** than any other brand.

Consumer Driver Usage by Model

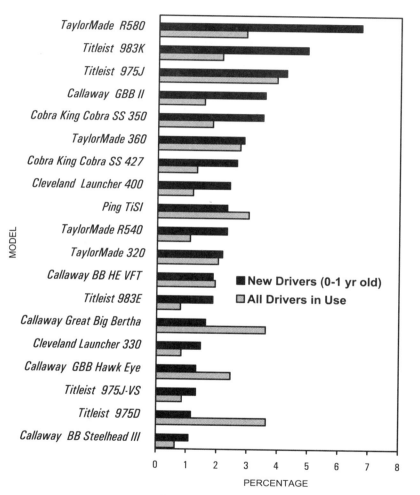

Percentage share of consumer equipment in use. Nationwide on-course
consumer survey conducted summer 2003; 3,151 respondents.

Our data reflects not only which clubs are hot this year, but also which clubs players continue to use over time.

The Titleist 975D, seen at the bottom of this graph, still accounts for nearly 4% of all drivers in use in the United States.

DRIVERS: WHAT CONSUMERS USE MOST

Driver Model Usage by Handicap

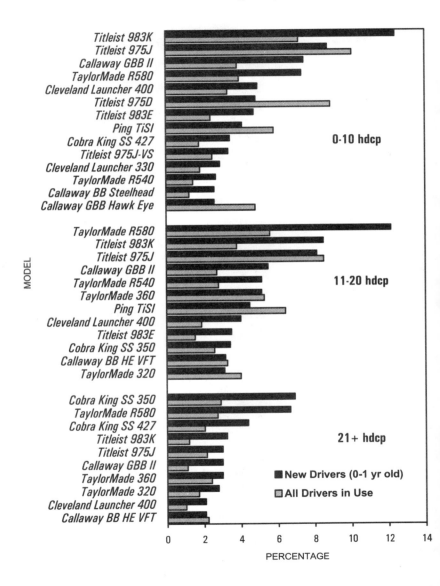

Percentage share of consumer equipment in use. Nationwide on-course
consumer survey conducted summer 2002; 3,151 respondents.

DRIVERS: WHAT CONSUMERS USE MOST

Driver Model Usage by Age

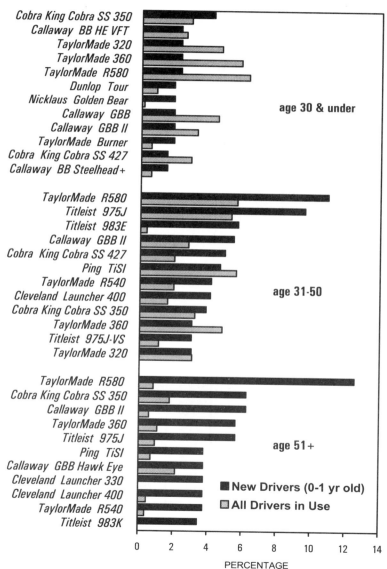

PERCENTAGE

Percentage share of consumer equipment in use. Nationwide on-course consumer survey conducted summer 2002; 3,151 respondents.

Not Too Long, Not Too Springy

The Great Driver War appears to be over. Late in 2003, the U.S. Golf Association added a new rule that effectively **stops the distance race** among drivers.

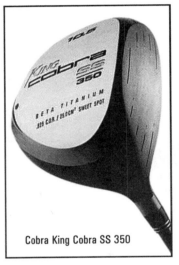

Cobra King Cobra SS 350

This rule limits the length of drivers to **48 inches**. The rule applies to all golf clubs except putters, so golfers can still use putters that are longer. than 48 inches.

Drivers longer than 48 inches, providing they were manufactured before Jan. 1, 2004, are grandfathered for one year under the new rule. Still, the rule effectively stops the proliferation of **super-long drivers**.

This rule is the same throughout the world, becuse the USGA and Royal & Ancient Golf Club of St. Andrews, Scotland, worked together to write it.

Differences remain, however, between drivers in the United States, Mexico and Canada and drivers in the rest of the world.

All drivers in countries that follow USGA rules now are limited to a specified length and coefficient of restitution (COR, or spring-like effect). The COR limit does not go into effect in the rest of the world (R & A jurisdiction) until January 1, 2008.

Cleveland Launcher

This COR restriction, which will be worldwide in four years, has largely stopped manufacturers from developing

new thin-faced drivers. As a driver face gets thinner, it has more flex or spring-like effect. As a result, the COR grows higher.

The COR limit of .830 was enacted in November, 1998, by the USGA. After several years or wrangling, the R & A finally agreed in 2002 to adopt the rule in 2008.

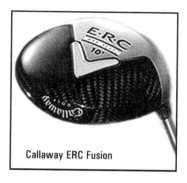

Callaway ERC Fusion

Nike Ignite 410

To see which drivers have failed the COR test administered by the USGA, visit *www.usga.org* and go the the Equipment section of the website to find the **nonconforming driver list,** which is updated weekly.

As stated by the USGA, the clubs appearing on this list "are **prohibited** from use in any round of golf in the United States and Mexico conducted under USGA Rules, including those rounds played for posting handicaps."

The USGA website also contains the list of conforming golf balls, as tested and approved to be in compliance with the Rules of Golf.

It isn't widely known, but there is a **minimum length** for golf clubs, too. That length is 18 inches.

The 18-inch rule was written to prevent golfers from being able to bump a putt with a sawed-off putter.

MAC Golf Powersphere

Darrell Golfer Satisfaction Ratings™
Driver Brands by Handicap

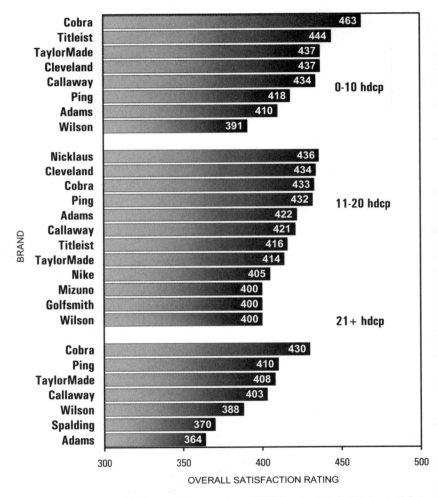

"How satisfied are you with your equipment?" 500 is most satisfied. 100 is least satisfied. 2,277 opinion respondents. (Minimum of 15 responses per subgroup for brands shown.)

The graph above represents consumer opinions of all models of a particular brand seen as a whole.

To see which models contributed to the high scores of those brands above, see *Model Satisfaction by Feature*, page 92.

DRIVERS: CONSUMER OPINIONS

Darrell Golfer Satisfaction Ratings™
Driver Models by Handicap

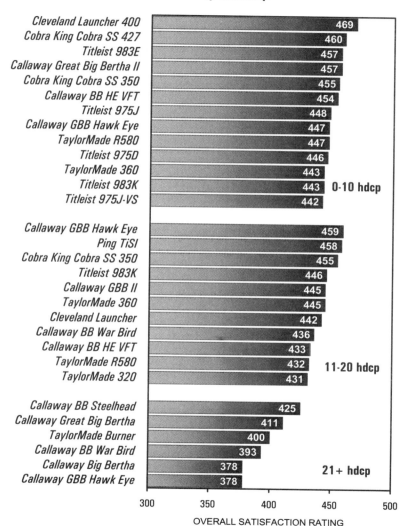

MODEL

0-10 hdcp
- Cleveland Launcher 400 — 469
- Cobra King Cobra SS 427 — 460
- Titleist 983E — 457
- Callaway Great Big Bertha II — 457
- Cobra King Cobra SS 350 — 455
- Callaway BB HE VFT — 454
- Titleist 975J — 448
- Callaway GBB Hawk Eye — 447
- TaylorMade R580 — 447
- Titleist 975D — 446
- TaylorMade 360 — 443
- Titleist 983K — 443
- Titleist 975J-VS — 442

11-20 hdcp
- Callaway GBB Hawk Eye — 459
- Ping TiSI — 458
- Cobra King Cobra SS 350 — 455
- Titleist 983K — 446
- Callaway GBB II — 445
- TaylorMade 360 — 445
- Cleveland Launcher — 442
- Callaway BB War Bird — 436
- Callaway BB HE VFT — 433
- TaylorMade R580 — 432
- TaylorMade 320 — 431

21+ hdcp
- Callaway BB Steelhead — 425
- Callaway Great Big Bertha — 411
- TaylorMade Burner — 400
- Callaway BB War Bird — 393
- Callaway Big Bertha — 378
- Callaway GBB Hawk Eye — 378

OVERALL SATISFACTION RATING (300 – 500)

"How satisfied are you with your equipment?" 500 is most satisfied. 100 is least satisfied. 2,277 opinion respondents. (Minimum of 12 responses per subgroup for models shown.)

Drivers

Consumer Opinions

Better players give higher scores to their equipment.

Darrell Golfer Satisfaction Ratings™
Driver Brands by Age

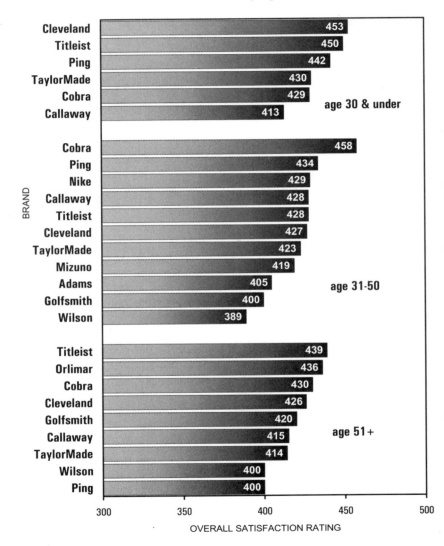

"How satisfied are you with your equipment?" 500 is most satisfied. 100 is least satisfied. Consumer golfers rate the equipment they are actually using the day of the survey. 2,277 opinion respondents. (Minimum of 15 responses per subgroup for brands shown.)

DRIVERS: CONSUMER OPINIONS

Darrell Golfer Satisfaction Ratings™
Driver Models by Age

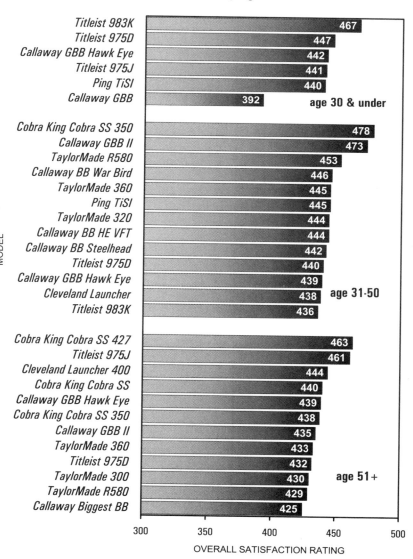

MODEL

age 30 & under

Titleist 983K	467
Titleist 975D	447
Callaway GBB Hawk Eye	442
Titleist 975J	441
Ping TiSI	440
Callaway GBB	392

age 31-50

Cobra King Cobra SS 350	478
Callaway GBB II	473
TaylorMade R580	453
Callaway BB War Bird	446
TaylorMade 360	445
Ping TiSI	445
TaylorMade 320	444
Callaway BB HE VFT	444
Callaway BB Steelhead	442
Titleist 975D	440
Callaway GBB Hawk Eye	439
Cleveland Launcher	438
Titleist 983K	436

age 51+

Cobra King Cobra SS 427	463
Titleist 975J	461
Cleveland Launcher 400	444
Cobra King Cobra SS	440
Callaway GBB Hawk Eye	439
Cobra King Cobra SS 350	438
Callaway GBB II	435
TaylorMade 360	433
Titleist 975D	432
TaylorMade 300	430
TaylorMade R580	429
Callaway Biggest BB	425

300   350   400   450   500

OVERALL SATISFACTION RATING

Drivers

Consumer Opinions

"How satisfied are you with your equipment?" 500 is most satisfied. 100 is least satisfied. Consumer golfers rate the equipment they are actually using the day of the survey. 2,277 opinion respondents. (Minimum of 12 responses per subgroup for brands/models shown.)

Darrell Golfer Satisfaction Ratings™
Driver Brands by Feature

—— Satisfaction SCORE by Equipment Feature ——

DRIVERS (*Listed Alphabetically*)	Overall	Distance	Accuracy	Feel	Value	Forgiveness
Average Score	*416*	*415*	*424*	*419*	*411*	*415*
Adams	395	402	398	398	390	376
Callaway	*420*	428	*419*	422	412	*417*
Cleveland	*432*	*447*	*435*	*431*	*421*	*432*
Cobra	*440*	*439*	*436*	*439*	*438*	*436*
Dunlop	336	352	340	344	360	336
Golfsmith	411	417	406	415	*443*	397
Knight	361	367	350	350	389	339
Mizuno	415	*431*	415	*427*	419	385
Nicklaus	416	419	413	425	419	409
Nike	408	426	413	411	403	408
Orlimar	413	417	404	409	*423*	387
Ping	*425*	*437*	*427*	*429*	416	*425*
Pro Select	353	353	342	347	374	347
Spalding	381	394	375	387	387	375
TaylorMade	*420*	429	*417*	426	*420*	415
Titleist	*433*	*443*	*435*	*432*	*421*	*423*
Wilson	394	400	395	396	404	393

"How satisfied are you with your equipment?" 500 is most satisfied. 100 is least satisfied. Consumer golfers rate the equipment they are actually using the day of the survey. 2,277 opinion respondents. (Minimum of 15 responses per subgroup for brands shown.)

❖ Compare each score to the average seen in the top row.
❖ Numbers in *bold italic* indicate top 5 scores in each category.
❖ Scores for individual models are listed on the opposite page.

Cleveland, Titleist and Cobra are among the Top Five drivers in **every satisfaction category**. TaylorMade, Callaway and Mizuno drivers are top-rated in multiple categories. Golfsmith and Orlimar score high in *value*.

Because manufacturers offer a variety of models, brand scores (*above*) do not correspond directly to model scores on the opposite page. Differences of only a few rating points are not statistically significant.

The Titleist 983K receives the highest rating in accuracy. (*See opposite.*)

DRIVERS: CONSUMER OPINIONS

Darrell Golfer Satisfaction Ratings™
Driver Models by Feature

—— Satisfaction SCORE by Equipment Feature ——

DRIVERS
(Listed Alphabetically)

	Overall	Distance	Accuracy	Feel	Value	Forgiveness
Average Score	*416*	*415*	*424*	*419*	*411*	*415*
Adams Tight Lies	400	404	407	400	389	385
Callaway BB Steelhead	416	432	424	434	413	413
Callaway BB HE VFT	445	431	431	422	437	425
Callaway Big Bertha	401	397	415	404	391	400
Callaway Big Bertha C4	382	406	376	365	382	347
Callaway Big Bertha War Bird	426	418	424	421	421	426
Callaway Biggest Big Bertha	421	426	443	425	417	412
Callaway GBB Hawk Eye	438	424	445	441	424	412
Callaway Great Big Bertha	410	412	412	421	410	408
Callaway Great Big Bertha II	*451*	445	*465*	445	*459*	432
Callaway Steelhead	427	441	435	440	422	430
Cleveland Launcher 400	*457*	*457*	455	*457*	*462*	*443*
Cobra King Cobra SS	*452*	*452*	*462*	*462*	443	*452*
Cobra King Cobra SS 350	*452*	*450*	453	*450*	*445*	*443*
Cobra King Cobra SS 427	*460*	*455*	450	*455*	*455*	*465*
Dunlop Tour	341	345	359	350	341	368
Mizuno T-Zoid	429	441	441	447	400	418
Orlimar TriMetal	412	400	412	406	388	429
Ping i3	428	428	439	433	428	406
Ping TiSI	440	445	455	443	*444*	429
TaylorMade 200	400	400	440	407	380	420
TaylorMade 320	433	427	438	429	427	*439*
TaylorMade 360	446	442	460	*450*	438	*439*
TaylorMade Burner	400	397	400	403	394	406
TaylorMade R540	437	424	447	429	437	419
TaylorMade R580	441	439	449	446	441	422
TaylorMade Ti Bubble 2	419	423	419	431	423	419
Titleist 975D	437	440	442	436	418	430
Titleist 975J-VS	437	437	*462*	431	437	425
Titleist 983E	*459*	*453*	*465*	447	435	424
Titleist 983K	444	446	*473*	446	439	427
Wilson Deep Red	400	404	400	409	404	414

*"How satisfied are you with your equipment?" 500 is most satisfied. 100 is least satisfied. Numbers in **bold italic** indicate top 5 scores for each category. Consumer golfers rate the equipment they are actually using the day of the survey. 2,277 opinion respondents. (Minimum of 12 responses per subgroup for models shown.)*

Drivers

Consumer Opinions

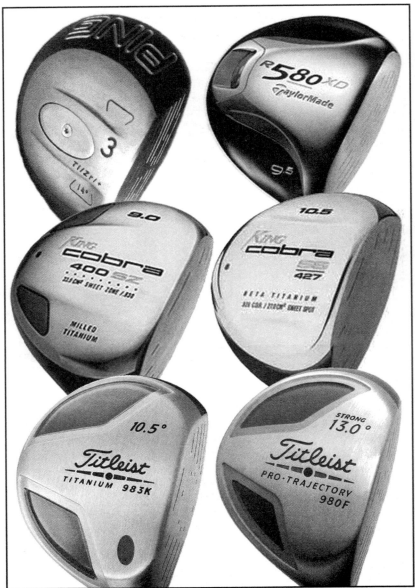

Images listed clockwise from top left: Ping TiSI, TaylorMade R580, Cobra King Cobra 4000SZ, Cobra King Cobra SS427, Titleist Pro Trajectory 980F & Titleist Titanium 983K.

Top Driver Models
At Major Amateur Events

U.S. Amateur
Titleist 983K
Titleist 983E
TaylorMade R540
TaylorMade R510
Titleist 975J
Titleist 975J.VS
Callaway GBB II PS
Cleveland Launcher 400
Ping Si3
TaylorMade 360

NCAA Div. 1 Men's
Titleist 983K
Callaway GBB II
Titleist 975J
Ping TiSI Tec
Callaway GBB II PS
TaylorMade R580
Titleist 975J.VS
Callaway HE VFT
TaylorMade 360

U.S. Boys Junior
Titleist 983K
Titleist 983E
Titleist 975J
TaylorMade R580
Callaway GBB II PS
Titleist 975J.VS
Taylormade R510
Titleist 975D
Titleist 975L.FE

U.S. Women's Amateur
Titleist 983K
Callaway GBB II
Titleist 975J
Ping TiSI Tec
Callaway GBB II PS
TaylorMade R580
Titleist 975J.VS
Callaway HE VFT
TaylorMade 360
Ping Si3

NCAA Women's
Ping TiSI Tec
Callaway GBB II
Titleist 975J
Callaway GBB II PS
TaylorMade R580
Titleist 983K
Callaway HE VFT PS
Henry-Griffitts 400
Titleist 975J.VS

U.S. Girls Junior
Titleist 983K
Callaway GBB II
Titleist 975J
TaylorMade 360
Ping TiSI Tec
TaylorMade R58
Cleveland Launcher 400
Titleist 975J.VS
Callaway GBB II PS

Drivers
Amateur Usage

These are the top driver models among competitive amateur golfers. Any of these drivers would make an excellent gift for a skilled golfer.

DRIVERS: HEAD SHOTS

From top to bottom: Nike 405, Yonex VMass 350, Precept Tour Premium, Callaway Big Bertha & Callaway HE VFT.

Tour - Drivers by Brand

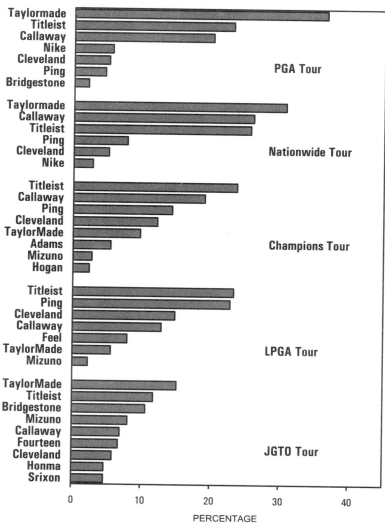

2003 Data. Sample size:
PGA 6,509 drivers; Champions 2,587; Nationwide 4,509; LPGA 3,977;
JGTO 3,339. Descending order of usage per tour.

TaylorMade wins the driver count on the 2003 PGA Tour.

PGA Tour - Drivers by Brand
Overall vs. Winners

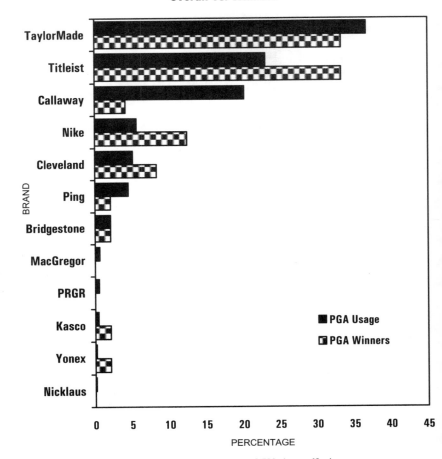

All 2003 PGA Tournaments. Sample size: 6,503 players; 48 winners.

All other driver brands used on PGA Tour in 2003: **Adams, Alpha Reaction, Cobra, Dunlop, La Jolla, M Golf, Nicklaus, Orlimar, Pax, Sonartec, Srixon, Wilson.**

In 2003, **TaylorMade** leads the PGA Tour in drivers. **Titleist** and **TaylorMade** each score the same number of wins.

Titleist's 983K model scores the most wins. *(See opposite page.)*

A brand's staff players for the most part use that brand's driver. See *Tournament Winners, pp. 205-206.*

PGA Tour - Drivers by Model
Overall vs. Winners

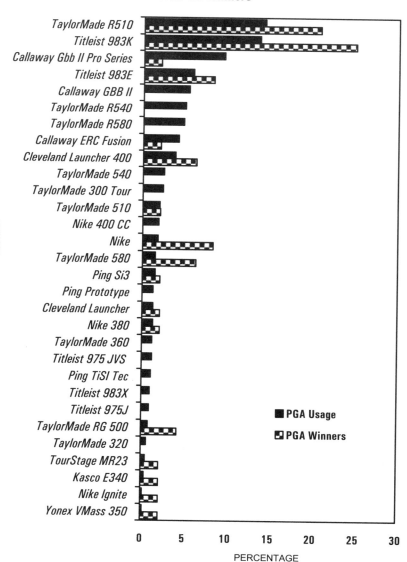

All 2003 PGA Tournaments. Sample size: 6,503 players; 48 winners.
Every model used to win a tournament is on this chart.

Champions Tour - Drivers by Brand
Overall vs. Winners

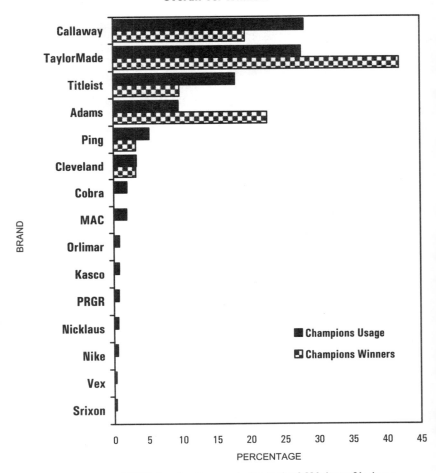

All 2003 Champions Tournaments. Sample size: 2,604 players; 31 winners.

*All other driver brands used on Champions Tour in 2003: **Golf Gear, Golfsmith, Hogan, Honma, Mchenry, Mizuno, Yonex.***

Callaway leads in driver usage on the Senior Tour in 2003, while TaylorMade racks up the most wins.

Adams Red Line Tour and TaylorMade R500 have the most wins of any model. *(See opposite page.)*

Champions Tour - Drivers by Model
Overall vs. Winners

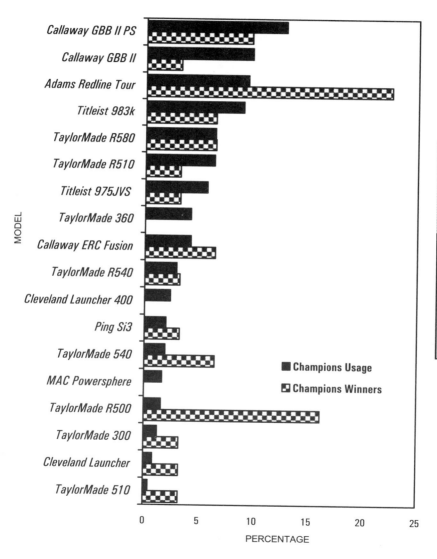

All 2003 Champions Tournaments. Sample size: 2,604 players; 31 winners.
Every model used to win a tournament is on this chart.

Nationwide Tour - Drivers by Brand
Overall vs. Winners

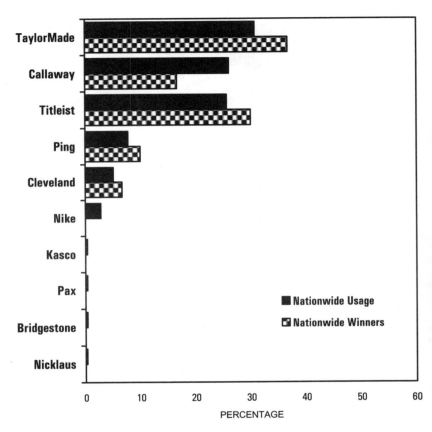

All 2003 Nationwide Tournaments. Sample size: 4,501 players; 30 winners.
All other driver brands used on Nationwide Tour in 2003: **Adams, Alpha, Cobra, Dunlop,**
E Lord, Feel, Golf Gear, Golfsmith, Henry-Griffits, KZG, MacGregor, Makser, Mizuno,
Nicklaus, Orlimar, PRGR, S Yard, Swing Sync, Wilson, Yonex.

TaylorMade leads in both driver usage and wins on the Nationwide
Tour in 2003. The brand's R510 model contributes to more wins than
any other.

Only five brands account for all winners.

Nationwide driver models mimic those of PGA Tour shares, but differ considerably from Champions and LPGA Tour shares.

Nationwide Tour - Drivers by Model
Overall vs. Winners

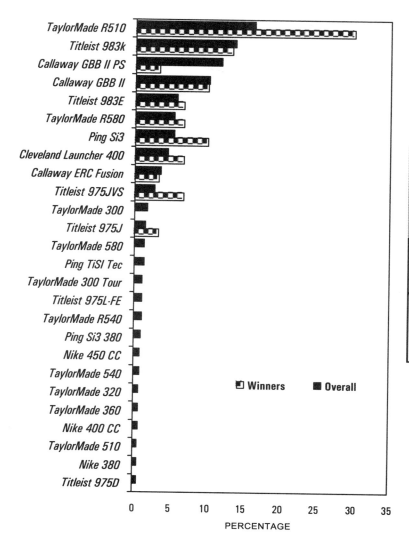

All 2003 Nationwide Tournaments. Sample size: 4,5010 players; 30 winners.
Every model used to win a tournament is on this chart..

DRIVERS: PRO USAGE

LPGA Tour - Drivers by Brand
Overall vs. Winners

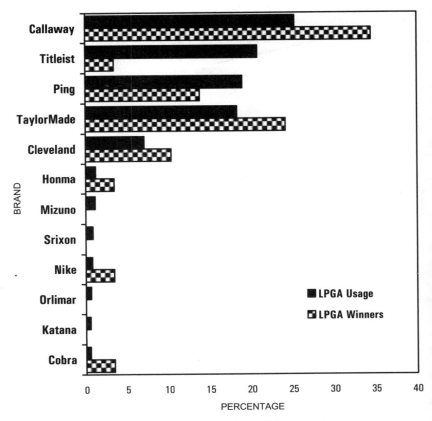

All 2003 LPGA Tournaments. Sample size: 3,850players; 29 winners.

*All other driver brands used on LPGA Tour in 2003: **Alpha, Bridgestone, E Lord, Feel, Golfsmith, Henry-Griffitts, Kasco, MAC, MacGregor, Makser, Nicklaus, S Yard, Yonex.***

Callaway drivers top both usage and wins on the LPGA tour in 2003.

The brand's Great Big Bertha Pro Series driver is the most popular model among the ladies, outpacing its rivals in victories.

See *Tournament Winner (pages 208-209)* to identify the LPGA Callaway staff players who won tournaments in 2003.

LPGA Tour - Drivers by Model
Overall vs. Winners

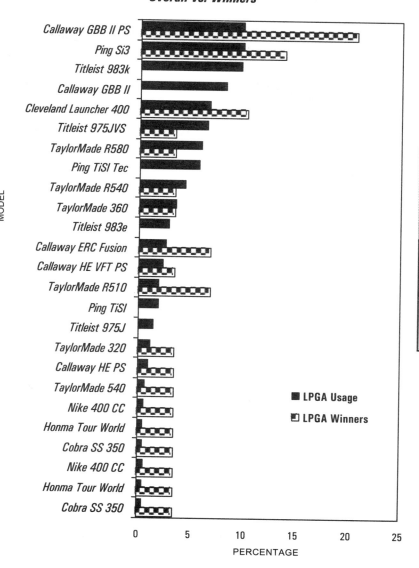

All 2003 LPGA Tournaments. Sample size: 3,850players; 29 winners.
Every model used to win a tournament is on this chart.

Japan Tour - Drivers by Brand
Overall vs. Winners

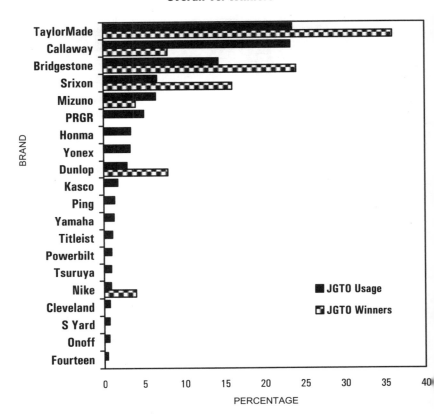

All 2003 JGTO Tournaments. Sample size: 3,343 players; 25 winners.

All other driver brands used on JGTO Tour in 2003: **Concept, Crews, Fourteen, Justick, Maruman, Tour Concept, Wilson.**

TaylorMade edges out Callaway in driver usage on the Japan Tour in 2003 as it captures the lion's share of wins.

Along with the TaylorMade R540, two Japanese models tie for the most number of wins: Srixon's W 201 and Bridgestone's X-Drive 300.

Japan Tour - Drivers by Model
Overall vs. Winners

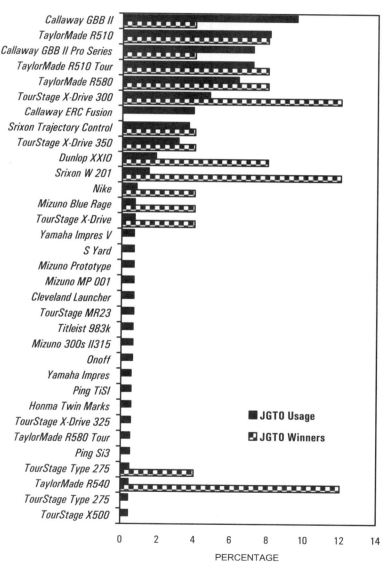

All 2003 LPGA Tournaments. Sample size: 3,343players; 25 winners.
Every model used to win a tournament is on this chart.

DRIVER SHAFTS: PRO USAGE

Tour - Driver Shafts by Brand
(Graphite & Steel)

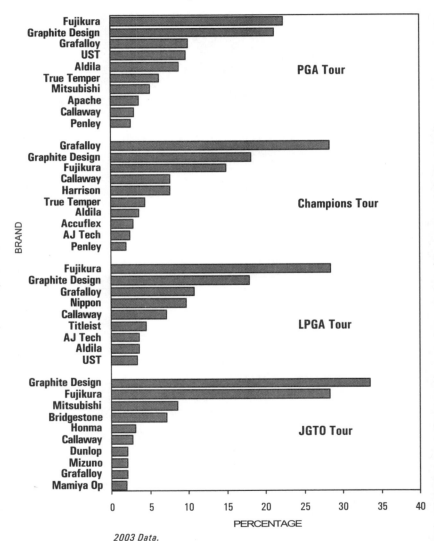

2003 Data.
Sample Sizes: PGA 6,502; Champions 2,603; LPGA 3,850; JGTO 3,368.

The above shafts are mostly graphite shafts. In contrast, most pros use *(see pg. 62).*

Tour - Driver Shafts by Model
(Graphite & Steel)

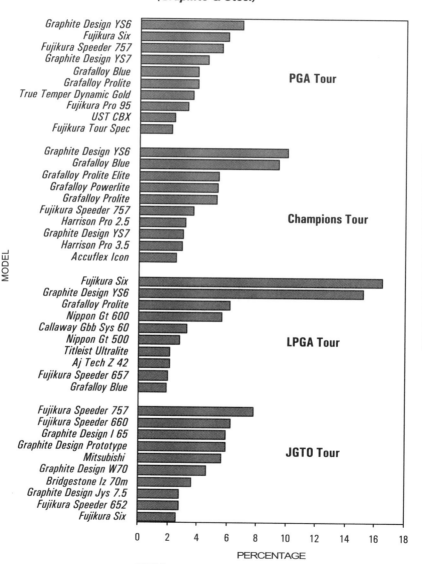

2003 Data.
Sample Sizes: PGA 6,502; Champions 2,603; LPGA 3,850; JGTO 3,368.

Tour - Driver Grips by Brand

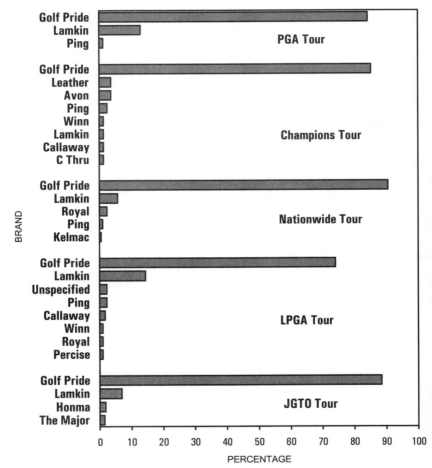

Descending order of leading brand usage for each tour. Leather grips are not surveyed by brand. 2003 data, selected events.

Golf Pride remains the dominant brand of driver grips in 2003.

Compare the uniformity of driver grip models to the relative diversity of putter grips, as seen on *pages 180-181*.

Tour - Driver Grips by Model

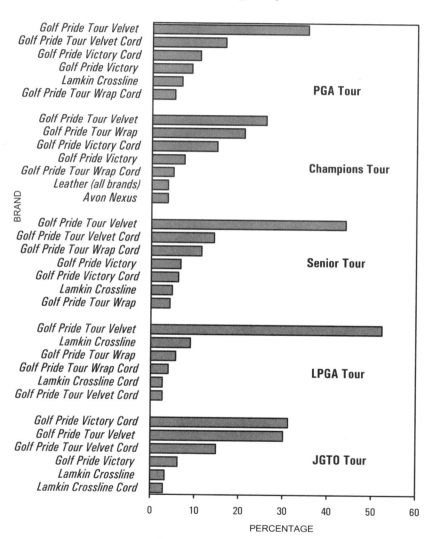

Descending order of leading model usage for each tour. Leather grips are not
surveyed by model. 2003 data, selected events.

Golf Pride's Tour Velvet driver grips top the U.S. professional tours,
while the Victory model is most used on the Japan Tour.

DRIVERS: PRO STATISTICS

2003 PGA Driver Statistics
For Brand and Model

Driver Brand and Model	# of Uses	Sum of Official Money $	Average Winnings per Use $	Average Driving Accuracy %	Average Driving Distance Yards
BRIDGESTONE					
T.STAGE MR23	34	1,812,936.00	56,654.25	64.888	278.301
J310	32	1,700,218.00	53,131.81	64.085	282.872
J340	20	176,047.00	8,802.35	59.643	276.319
T.STAGE TYPE 275	17	56,088.00	3,299.29	60.706	282.383
X-DRIVE 300	14	251,775.00	17,983.93	52.779	283.591
TOUR STAGE Z340	5	262,170.00	52,434.00	65.357	288.675
X-DRIVE	3	13,988.00	4,662.67	45.238	274.875
TOUR STAGE	1	72,000.00	72,000.00	60.714	290
X-DRIVE 325	1	53,000.00	53,000.00	46.429	312.375
TYPE 350	1	7,600.00	7,600.00	58.929	288.875
Sum/Average of All Models	135	4,405,822.00	33,126.48	60.982	281.133
CALLAWAY					
GBB II PROSERIES	619	12,452,795.00	20,685.71	58.697	283.745
GBB II	349	7,939,662.00	23,283.47	60.765	282.962
ERC FUSION	271	4,922,151.00	18,574.15	60.737	288.107
HE VFT TS	32	1,439,133.00	44,972.91	58.736	294.541
HE PS	28	432,418.00	16,015.48	65.206	299.071
GREAT BIG BERTHA	8	144,430.00	20,632.86	47.098	283.292
HE VFT PS	6	10,035.00	1,672.50	56.845	278.229
HE VFT	1	29,849.00	29,849.00	0	0
Sum/Average of All Models	1314	27,370,473.00	21,366.49	59.682	285.027

2003 Season, all PGA tournaments for which statistics are available. Not all brands and models are listed above. Brand and overall sums and averages, however, do include all models and brands surveyed.1 yard = 0.914 meters. $ = US Dollars.

n.a. indicates drivers used at tournaments for which no accuracy/distance statistics are available.

Money statistics are derived from PGA "official money" data; players failing to make the cut are averaged with zero earnings. Driving distance reflects the PGA "measured drives" statistic; driving accuracy is computed from the PGA "fairways hit" statistic. Cut players' driving distance and accuracy for rounds completed are included in the above averages.

2003 PGA Driver Statistics
For Brand and Model

Driver Brand and Model	# of Uses	Sum of Official Money $	Average Winnings per Use $	Average Driving Accuracy %	Average Driving Distance Yards
CLEVELAND					
LAUNCHER 400	245	13,198,356.00	55,223.25	63.149	287.666
LAUNCHER	85	5,793,220.00	70,649.02	60.225	283.176
400	1	27,625.00	27,625.00	75	265.25
PROTOTYPE	1	9,090.00	9,090.00	82.143	288.875
LAUNCHER 460	1	6,780.00	6,780.00	75	287.75
Sum/Average of All Models	333	19,035,071.00	58,750.22	62.542	286.493
DUNLOP					
XXIO	3	29,849.00	9,949.67	54.762	268.625
XXIO T SPEC	2	61,650.00	30,825.00	67.857	264.375
Sum/Average of All Models	5	91,499.00	18,299.80	58.036	267.208
KASCO					
E340	25	2,001,561.00	83,398.38	67.074	280.645
Sum/Average of All Models	29	2,001,561.00	71,484.32	64.719	281.426
M GOLF					
Sum/Average of All Models	3	52,000.00	17,333.33	47.321	304.938
MACGREGOR					
V FOIL	20	1,028,082.00	54,109.58	58.198	284.898
V FOIL 350CC	9	19,860.00	2,206.67	73.23	287.736
EYEOMATIC	4	174,990.00	43,747.50	60.886	287.344
TOURNEY V CAVITY	3	64,189.00	21,396.33	56.548	279.083
TOURNEY 340CC	3	48,100.00	16,033.33	38.452	289.438
Sum/Average of All Models	39	1,335,221.00	35,137.39	60.297	285.647
MIZUNO					
MP 001	3	25,400.00	12,700.00	56.822	278.042
BLUE RAGE	2	31,083.00	15,541.50	58.929	293.938
Sum/Average of All Models	10	56,483.00	6,275.89	45.975	277.125

Here are the actual money and performance statistics from 2003 PGA Tour usage of major driver models.

Averages are less reliable for models with fewer than 100 uses.

2003 PGA Driver Statistics
For Brand and Model

Driver Brand and Model	# of Uses	Sum of Official Money $	Average Winnings per Use $	Average Driving Accuracy %	Average Driving Distance Yards
NICKLAUS					
AIR MAX	10	32,300.00	3,230.00	60.536	271.438
Sum/Average of All Models	10	32,300.00	3,230.00	60.536	271.438
NIKE					
400 CC	121	1,786,498.00	15,139.81	57.802	284.056
380	84	2,134,865.00	26,685.81	62.842	285.75
IGNITE	16	1,700,029.00	106,251.81	62.929	288.563
300 CC	9	190,103.00	23,762.88	64.955	285.375
PROTOTYPE	9	106,446.00	11,827.33	56.548	280.236
410	3	112,840.00	37,613.33	73.095	289.308
450 CC	2	114,350.00	57,175.00	72.321	266.5
330 CC	1	9,315.00	9,315.00	51.786	289.25
Sum/Average of All Models	366	12,840,659.00	36,170.87	60.55	283.897
PAX					
Sum/Average of All Models	8	35,531.00	4,441.38	67.96	292
PING					
SI3	97	5,138,117.00	54,660.82	60.776	282.688
PROTOTYPE	87	2,219,106.00	26,107.13	60.58	284.709
TISI TEC	70	2,453,869.00	35,055.27	62.358	287.795
SI3 380	20	514,718.00	25,735.90	66.591	281.961
SI3 340	11	969,904.00	88,173.09	63.189	287.839
ISI	10	250,449.00	25,044.90	55.783	284.319
Sum/Average of All Models	295	11,546,163.00	39,814.36	61.418	284.696
PRGR					
TR 340	21	553,576.00	26,360.76	66.098	287.345
CFM TR FORGED	7	216,165.00	30,880.71	58.854	291.521
Sum/Average of All Models	34	782,568.00	23,714.18	59.927	287.258
SRIXON					
Sum/Average of All Models	3	10,176.00	3,392.00	43.132	270.938
TAYLORMADE					
R510	932	34,806,739.00	38,375.68	60.881	286.192
R540	328	9,550,458.00	29,567.98	60.895	285.401
R580	312	5,668,588.00	18,708.21	58.865	285.566

2003 PGA Driver Statistics
For Brand and Model

Driver Brand and Model	# of Uses	Sum of Official Money $	Average Winnings per Use $	Average Driving Accuracy %	Average Driving Distance Yards
TAYLORMADE					
540	162	3,902,305.00	25,176.16	63.308	282.007
300 TOUR	155	5,479,550.00	36,049.67	62.263	285.748
510	128	4,991,402.00	39,302.38	58.913	287.746
580	98	7,766,414.00	80,066.12	55.987	282.932
360	79	3,250,800.00	42,218.18	61.517	285.099
RG500	51	3,327,804.00	67,914.37	56.845	290.809
320	36	1,189,944.00	33,054.00	59.906	284.567
300	30	481,386.00	16,599.52	55.712	283.142
320 TOUR	26	793,684.00	30,526.31	65.204	284.966
R510 TOUR	21	48,770.00	2,322.38	65.755	281.604
R580 XD	17	477,345.00	28,079.12	64.11	285.628
R540 XD	9	153,263.00	17,029.22	57.341	291.949
Sum/Average of All Models	2385	81,888,452.00	35,160.35	60.533	285.603
TITLEIST					
983K	893	35,898,598.00	41,357.83	59.628	285.42
983E	384	16,719,637.00	45,066.41	60.442	286.43
975JVS	75	2,763,153.00	37,851.41	56.251	283.616
983X	65	3,839,927.00	59,998.86	56.763	287.184
975J	57	1,874,074.00	32,878.49	55.294	281.333
975LFE	14	213,783.00	16,444.85	49.358	290.386
975D	5	682,250.00	136,450.00	61.786	302.125
975LFF	5	37,063.00	7,412.60	36.63	292.875
Sum/Average of All Models	1503	62,028,485.00	42,456.18	59.15	285.601
WILSON					
DEEP RED	6	424,735.00	70,789.17	52.679	287.15
FAT SHAFT	3	632,000.00	210,666.67	72.321	293
Sum/Average of All Models	9	1,056,735.00	117,415.00	57.589	288.821
YONEX					
VMASS 350	11	1,198,249.00	119,824.90	61.923	277.75
Sum/Average of All Models	12	1,198,249.00	108,931.73	62.787	278.455

Averages are less reliable for models with fewer than 100 uses.

Drivers

Tour

Statistics

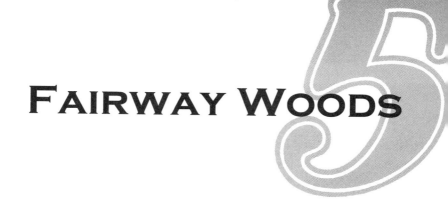

FAIRWAY WOODS

Chapter 5

FAIRWAY WOODS: OVERVIEW

How many fairway woods do golfers use? As seen in this graph, the answers can vary widely.

As it turns out, the average **PGA Tour** pro uses slightly more fairway woods than **the 0-5 handicap consumers** in our latest survey. And **LPGA** players are using nearly three fairway woods at each tournament, compared to just more than two for **female** consumers.

PGA	
Champions	
Nationwide	
LPGA	
Japan Golf Tour	
Consumer: Male	
Female	
0-5 hdcp	
6-10 hdcp	
11-15 hdcp	
16-20 hdcp	
21+ hdcp	

# of Fairway Woods per Player

Recreational golfers might do well to take a cue from the pros and **try another fairway wood** in their bag.

One notable PGA player uses a 3-wood and a 7-wood at every tournament. His name? **Vijay Singh**—who just happens to be the top money winner for the 2003 season.

There are certainly plenty of innovative fairway woods to choose from. For consumers, the biggest brands remain **Callaway** and **TaylorMade,** but this year both **Cobra** and **Cleveland** made substantial gains, surpassing **Titleist, Adams** and **Ping** fairway woods in new usage *(page 124).*

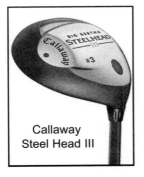

Callaway
Steel Head III

Some of the most-used consumer models include the Callaway Steelhead III, the Cleveland Launcher, Callaway King Cobra SS, TaylorMade V Steel and Titleist 975F.

In GOLFER SATISFACTION RATINGS, consumers rank the Titleist PT and 980F, the Ping i3, Cleveland Quadpro, and Callaway Great Big Bertha II and BB Steelhead+ tops for overall satisfaction *(see page 133).*

FAIRWAY WOODS: OVERVIEW

Taylormade
V Steel

The pros go for **TaylorMade** and **Callaway** fairway woods, with the former brand leading the PGA and Nationwide Tour, the latter the Champions Tour, LPGA and Japan Golf Tours *(see p. 137.)*

The wide range of fairway wood models used by tournament winners include the TaylorMade 200 Tour and V Steel, Callaway Steelhead III, Titleist 980F, Sonartec BBD and SS-03, Nike T40, Cleveland Quadpro, Adams Redline Tour, Ping TiSI Tec and i3, TourStage MR23 and F-ST, and Kasco Power Tornado *(see pages 139 to 147)*.

In shafts, the **steel True Temper Dynamic Gold** is a leading model on the PGA and Nationwide Tours. 16.8% of PGA fairway wood shafts are steel, compared to only 5.2% of the driver shafts.

Popular pro graphite shafts for fairway woods include Fujikura Pro 95 and Speeder 757, Graphite Design YS7, Grafalloy Prolite and UST Accra 75 *(pages 148-149)*.

In contrast with the variations seen between fairway and driver shafts, **grips** for fairway woods are nearly identitical to those for drivers on the pro tours. The Golf Pride Tour Velvet is the predominant choice *(pages 150-151)*.

Fairway

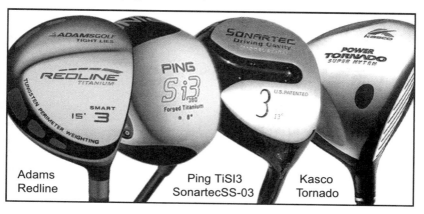

Adams
Redline

Ping TiSI3
SonartecSS-03

Kasco
Tornado

FAIRWAY WOODS: WHAT CONSUMERS USE MOST

Consumer Fairway Wood Usage by Brand

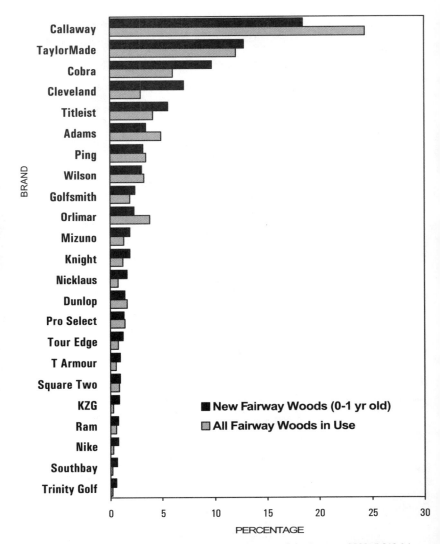

Nationwide on-course consumer survey conducted summer 2003; 5,912 fairway woods surveyed.

Callaway leads in both new (black bar) and total (gray bar) fairway woods usage.

FAIRWAY WOODS: WHAT CONSUMERS USE MOST

Consumer Fairway Wood Usage by Model

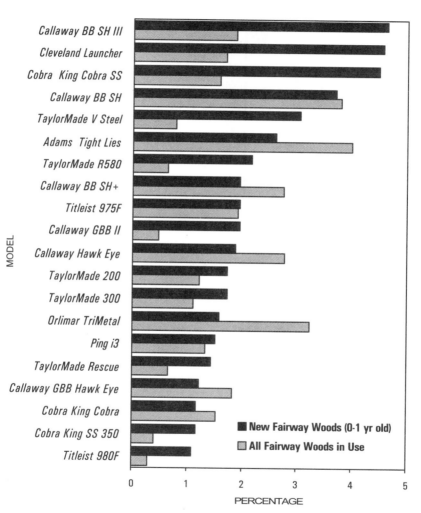

Percentage share of consumer equipment in use.
Nationwide on-course consumer survey conducted summer 2003;
1,380 respondents for "New Fairway Woods" and 5,912 respondents for
"All Fairway Woods".

Callaway's new Steelhead III, Cleveland's Launcher and the Cobra SS
are the most popular new fairway wood models.

Fairway Wood Model Usage by Handicap

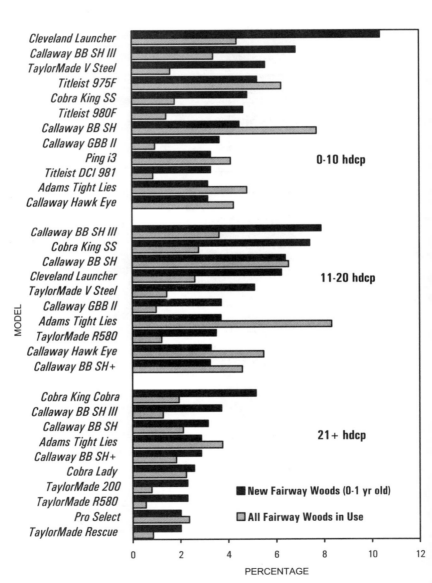

Percentage share of consumer equipment in use. Nationwide on-course consumer survey conducted summer 2003; 5,912 fairway woods surveyed.

FAIRWAY WOODS: WHAT CONSUMERS USE MOST

Fairway Wood Model Usage by Age

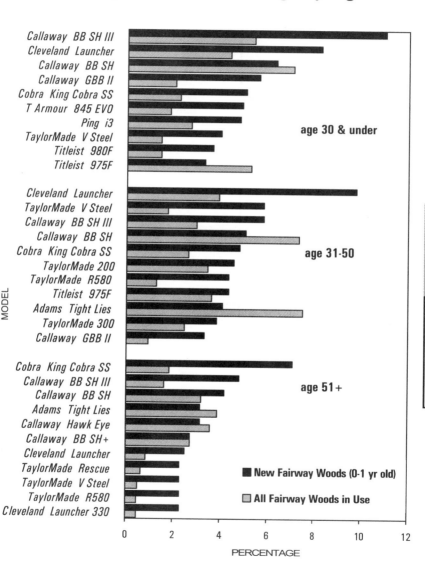

Percentage share of consumer equipment in use. Nationwide on-course consumer survey conducted summer 2003; 1,357 respondents for "New Fairway Woods" and 5,797 respondents for "All Fairway Woods".

Darrell Golfer Satisfaction Ratings™
Fairway Woods Brands by Handicap

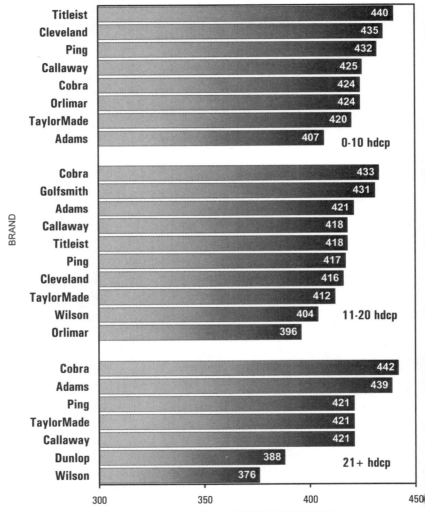

Brand	0-10 hdcp
Titleist	440
Cleveland	435
Ping	432
Callaway	425
Cobra	424
Orlimar	424
TaylorMade	420
Adams	407

Brand	11-20 hdcp
Cobra	433
Golfsmith	431
Adams	421
Callaway	418
Titleist	418
Ping	417
Cleveland	416
TaylorMade	412
Wilson	404
Orlimar	396

Brand	21+ hdcp
Cobra	442
Adams	439
Ping	421
TaylorMade	421
Callaway	421
Dunlop	388
Wilson	376

OVERALL SATISFACTION RATING

"How satisfied are you with your equipment?" 500 is most satisfied. 100 is least satisfied. Consumer golfers rate the equipment they are actually using the day of the survey. 2,265 opinion respondents. (Minimum of 10 responses per subgroup for brands shown.)

Satisfaction charts record consumer *opinions*.

FAIRWAY WOODS: CONSUMER OPINIONS

Darrell Golfer Satisfaction Ratings™
Fairway Woods Models by Handicap

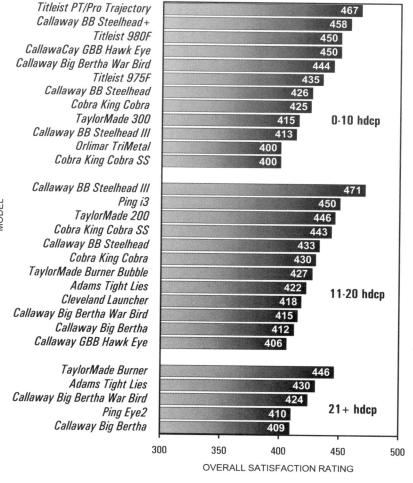

MODEL

0-10 hdcp

Model	Rating
Titleist PT/Pro Trajectory	467
Callaway BB Steelhead+	458
Titleist 980F	450
CallawaCay GBB Hawk Eye	450
Callaway Big Bertha War Bird	444
Titleist 975F	435
Callaway BB Steelhead	426
Cobra King Cobra	425
TaylorMade 300	415
Callaway BB Steelhead III	413
Orlimar TriMetal	400
Cobra King Cobra SS	400

11-20 hdcp

Model	Rating
Callaway BB Steelhead III	471
Ping i3	450
TaylorMade 200	446
Cobra King Cobra SS	443
Callaway BB Steelhead	433
Cobra King Cobra	430
TaylorMade Burner Bubble	427
Adams Tight Lies	422
Cleveland Launcher	418
Callaway Big Bertha War Bird	415
Callaway Big Bertha	412
Callaway GBB Hawk Eye	406

21+ hdcp

Model	Rating
TaylorMade Burner	446
Adams Tight Lies	430
Callaway Big Bertha War Bird	424
Ping Eye2	410
Callaway Big Bertha	409

OVERALL SATISFACTION RATING

Fairway

Consumer Opinions

"How satisfied are you with your equipment?" 500 is most satisfied. 100 is least satisfied. Consumer golfers rate the equipment they are actually using the day of the survey. 2,265 opinion respondents. (Minimum of 12 responses per subgroup for models shown.)

Two older models, the Titleist PT and the TaylorMade Burner, remain favorites among low- and high-handicaps.

Darrell Golfer Satisfaction Ratings™
Fairway Woods Brands by Age

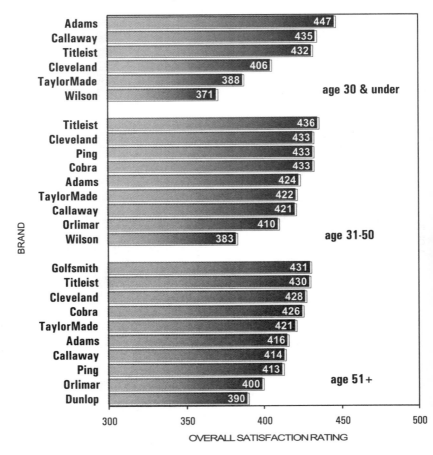

"How satisfied are you with your equipment?" 500 is most satisfied. 100 is least satisfied. Consumer golfers rate the equipment they are actually using the day of the survey. 2,265 opinion respondents. (Minimum of 12 responses per subgroup for brands shown.)

Ping i3 fairway woods are the top-rated model among golfers age 31 and up *(see opposite page)*. To see a detailed breakdown of opinions regarding fairway wood models, *please see page 133.*

Golfsmith received high scores among older players, yet no individual moel had a high enough sample size to appear on the opposite page.

Darrell Golfer Satisfaction Ratings™
Fairway Woods Models by Age

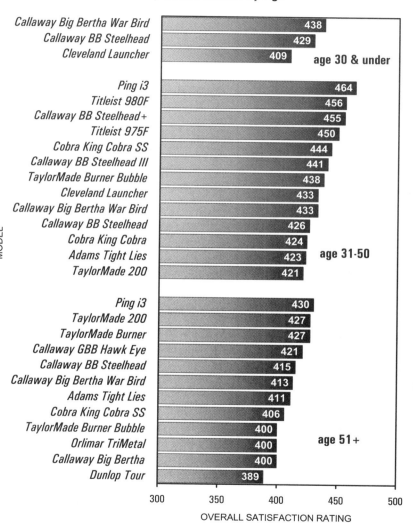

"How satisfied are you with your equipment?" 500 is most satisfied. 100 is least satisfied. Consumer golfers rate the equipment they are actually using the day of the survey. 2,265 opinion respondents. (Minimum of 12 responses per subgroup for brands/models shown.)

Darrell Golfer Satisfaction Ratings™
Fairway Woods Brands by Feature

—— Satisfaction SCORE by Equipment Feature ——

FAIRWAY WOODS (Listed Alphabetically)	Overall	Distance	Accuracy	Feel	Value	Forgiveness
Average Score	*411*	*415*	*413*	*415*	*412*	*405*
Adams	*423*	422	418	423	*422*	*419*
Callaway	420	*424*	*422*	*425*	417	414
Cleveland	*423*	*434*	*426*	*428*	417	*417*
Cobra	*430*	*433*	*429*	427	*432*	*427*
Dunlop	378	396	387	383	378	365
Golfsmith	419	419	419	420	*427*	*415*
MacGregor	387	400	387	387	*440*	373
Mizuno	369	400	387	387	375	356
Nicklaus	375	394	381	406	375	375
Orlimar	409	413	408	421	409	404
Ping	*423*	413	421	*424*	413	*415*
Spalding	362	381	369	362	369	337
TaylorMade	415	*429*	*422*	423	415	408
Titleist	*431*	*433*	*430*	*426*	*428*	*419*
Wilson	378	387	389	379	397	371

"How satisfied are you with your equipment?" 500 is most satisfied. 100 is least satisfied. Consumer golfers rate the equipment they are actually using the day of the survey. 2,265 opinion respondents. (Minimum of 15 responses per subgroup for brands shown.)

❖ Compare each score to the average seen in the top row.

❖ Numbers in ***bold italic*** indicate top 5 scores in each category.

❖ Scores for individual models are listed on the opposite page.

Titleist and **Cobra** fairway woods receive the highest overall consumer satisfaction ratings by brand in 2003, followed by **Ping** and **Adams**.

Scoring the highest overall satisfaction score by model are Ping i3, Callaway Great Big Bertha II, Cleveland Quadpro and the Titleist 980F and Pro Trajectory models *(see opposite page).*

TaylorMade V Steel is ranked highly for accuracy, feel and value.

Difference of only a few rating points are not statisticlly significant.

FAIRWAY WOODS: CONSUMER OPINIONS

Darrell Golfer Satisfaction Ratings™
Fairway Woods Models by Feature

—— Satisfaction SCORE by Equipment Feature ——

FAIRWAY WOODS (Listed Alphabetically)	Overall	Distance	Accuracy	Feel	Value	Forgive-ness
Average Score	*411*	*415*	*413*	*415*	*412*	*405*
Adams Tight Lies	423	423	421	427	421	419
Callaway BB HE VFT	427	436	436	*455*	418	410
Callaway BB Steelhead	429	433	427	435	425	418
Callaway BB Steelhead III	435	440	431	434	429	429
Callaway BB Steelhead+	437	*448*	*444*	446	*433*	425
Callaway Big Bertha War Bird	427	429	432	429	424	422
Callaway GBB Hawk Eye	421	429	418	426	418	415
Callaway Great Big Bertha II	*440*	*460*	*450*	*460*	430	*450*
Callaway Hawk Eye	421	429	421	432	417	411
Cleveland Launcher	424	435	430	430	416	422
Cleveland Quadpro	*442*	*450*	442	442	*442*	*442*
Cobra King Cobra	430	429	436	421	430	422
Cobra King Cobra SS	426	433	422	430	415	426
Dunlop Tour	379	400	390	390	379	368
Nicklaus Golden Bear	373	391	373	400	364	364
Orlimar TriMetal	407	410	402	420	407	405
Ping Eye2	406	394	419	406	412	387
Ping i3	*450*	436	*450*	*459*	432	*450*
Ping TiSI	433	447	433	433	400	*433*
TaylorMade 200	413	447	427	427	420	410
TaylorMade 300	410	414	410	414	410	405
TaylorMade Burner	417	426	423	417	410	409
TaylorMade R500	412	429	412	424	412	429
TaylorMade R580	414	421	414	429	421	*429*
TaylorMade V Steel	430	440	*450*	*470*	*440*	410
Titleist 975F	429	432	425	421	432	407
Titleist 980F	*447*	*459*	441	*453*	*435*	429
Titleist PT/Pro Trajectory	*440*	*460*	*453*	427	*447*	*433*
Wilson Deep Red	400	420	400	400	400	390

*"How satisfied are you with your equipment?" 500 is most satisfied. 100 is least satisfied. Numbers in **bold italic** indicate top 5 scores for each category. Consumer golfers rate the equipment they are actually using the day of the survey. 2,265 opinion respondents. (Minimum 10 responses per subgroup for brands/models shown.)*

Because this chart shows only the most common models, the brand satisfaction scores on the opposite page do not correlate directly to the model scores above.

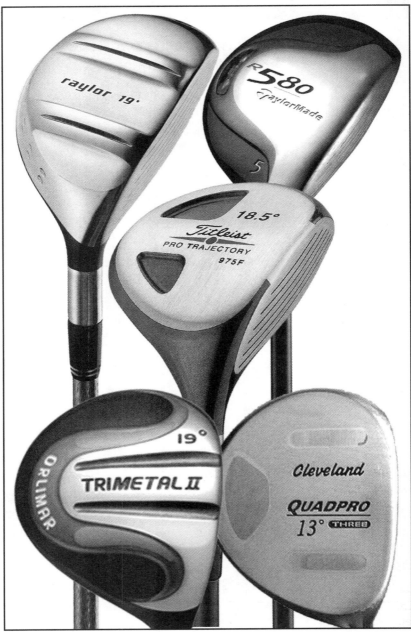

Images clockwise from top left: TaylorMade Raylor, TaylorMade R580, Titleist 975F, Cleveland Quadpro &, Orlimar TriMetal II.

FAIRWAY WOODS: AMATEUR USAGE

Top Fairway Wood Models
At Major Amateur Events

U.S. AMATEUR
Callaway Steelhead III
Callaway Steelhead Plus
Titleist 975F
Titleist PT
TaylorMade 200
TaylorMade Rescue
Titleist 980F
Callaway Steelhead
Ping TiSI Tec
TaylorMade V

U.S. WOMEN'S AMATEUR
Callaway Steelhead Plus
Callaway Steelhead III
Ping i3
Callaway Steelhead
Callaway HE
Titleist 975F
Cleveland Launcher
Callaway HE VFT
Ping TiSI Tec
TaylorMade 200

NCAA DIV. 1 MEN'S
Callaway Steelhead III
Ping TiSI Tec
TaylorMade 200
Callaway Steelhead Plus
TaylorMade 200 Tour
Titleist PT
Cleveland Launcher
TaylorMade Retro
Titleist 980F
Titleist 970 Series
Bridgestone 160F

NCAA WOMEN'S
Callaway Steelhead Plus
Callaway Steelhead III
Ping TiSI Tec
Callaway Steelhead
Callaway HE
Callaway HE VFT
Ping i3
Callaway WB
Cleveland Launcher
Titleist 975F
Cleveland Quadpro

U.S. BOYS JUNIOR
Callaway Steelhead Plus
Titleist 975F
Titleist 980F CR
Callaway Steelhead
Callaway Steelhead III
Sonartec
Titleist PT
TaylorMade Rescue
TaylorMade 200
Cleveland Launcher

U.S. GIRLS JUNIOR
Callaway Steelhead
Callaway Steelhead Plus
Callaway Steelhead III
Ping i3
Callaway HE
TaylorMade 200
Titleist 975F
Cleveland Launcher
Callaway GBB II

2003 Data. Listed in order of decreasing usage at each tournament.

Callaway Steelhead series fairway woods are top picks at major amateur tournaments in the U.S.

These models would be excellent choices for the skilled younger golfer shopping for a new fairway wood.

Fairway

Amateur Usage

FAIRWAY WOODS: GALLERY

(Images clockwise from top left) Ping i3, Sonartec NP-99,
TourStage z150, PRGR TR-X & Cobra King Cobra SS

FAIRWAY WOODS: PRO USAGE

Tour - Fairway Woods by Brand

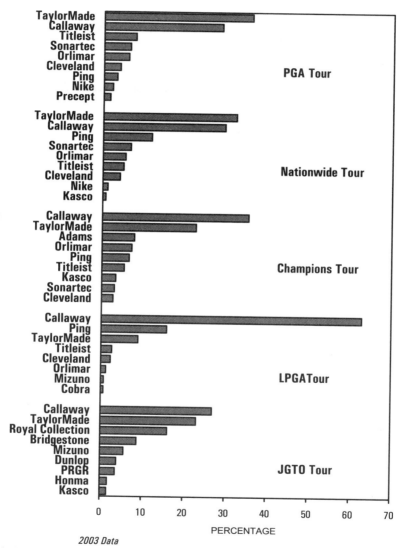

2003 Data

While TaylorMade brand fairway woods edge out Callaway on the PGA and Nationwide Tours in 2003, Callaway leads on the LPGA, Champions and Japan Golf Tours.

PGA Tour - Fairway Woods by Brand
Overall vs. Winners

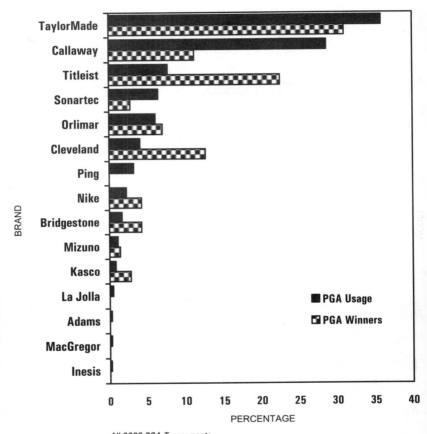

All 2003 PGA Tournaments.
Sample size: 10,482 fairway woods; 71 winners' fairway woods.

All other fairway wood brands used on PGA Tour in 2003: **Alpha Reaction, Catapult, Chipshot, Cobra, Dunlop, Nicklaus, Pax, Perfect, PRGR, Snake Eyes, Srixon, Top-Flite, Wilson.**

TaylorMade and **Callaway** show strong fairway wood usage on the PGA Tour in 2003.

Titleist and Clevelandfairway woods rack up a high percentage of wins.

See *Winners' Staff Affiliations, pp. 205-206.*

FAIRWAY WOODS: PRO USAGE

PGA Tour - Fairway Woods by Model
Overall vs. Winners

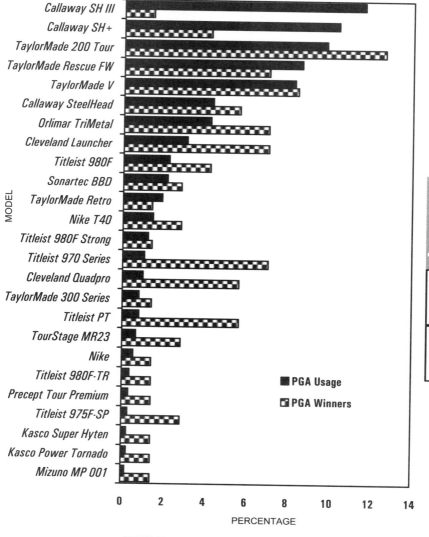

All 2003 PGA Tournaments.
Sample size: 10,482 fairway woods; 71 winners' fairway woods.
Every model used to win a tournament is on this chart.

Champions Tour - Fairway Woods by Brand
Overall vs. Winners

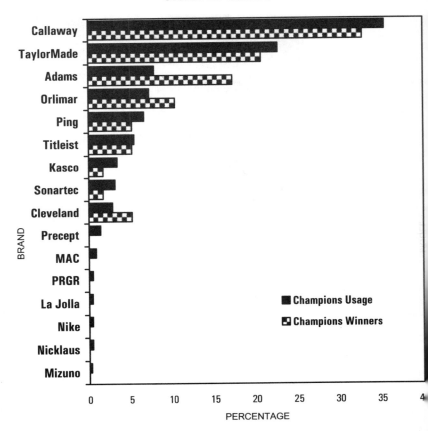

All 2003 ChampionsTournaments. Sample size: 5,398 fairway woods; 58 winners' fairway woods.

All other fairway wood brands used on Champions Tour in 2003:
Cobra, Dunlop, Excedo, Founders Club, GolfGear, Head, Kunnan, KZG, Maxfli, McHenry Metals, Perfect, Snake Eyes, Srixon, Top-Flite, Tour Edge, Wilson, Yonex.

Callaway, TaylorMade, Adams, Orlimar and **Ping** rank one to five in both usage and winners on the Champions Tour in 2003.

TaylorMade's 200 Tour scores a high percentage of wins.

Champions Tour - Fairway Woods by Model
Overall vs. Winners

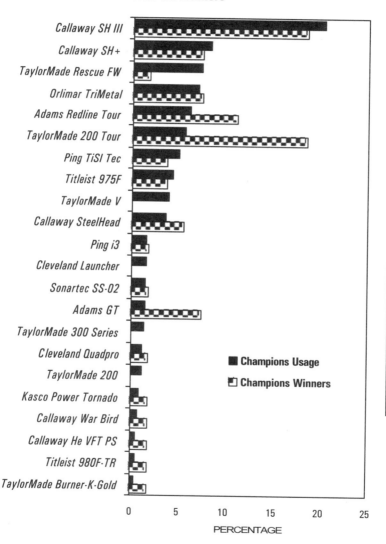

All 2003 Champions Tournaments.
Sample size: 5,398 fairway woods; 53 winners' fairway woods.
Every model used to win a tournament is on this chart.

FAIRWAY WOODS: PRO USAGE

Nationwide Tour - Fairway Woods by Brand
Overall vs. Winners

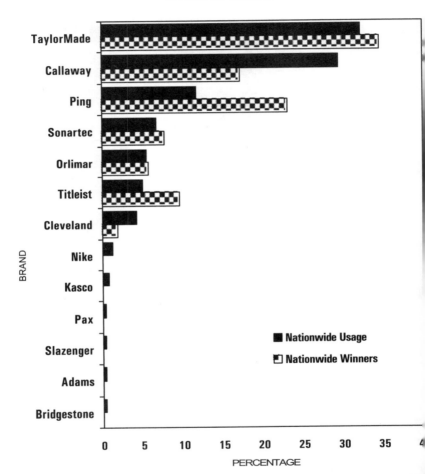

All 2003 Nationwide Tournaments. Sample size: 7,017 fairway woods; 52 winners' fai
way woods. Every model used to win a tournament is on this chart. All other fairwa
wood brands used on PGA Tour in 2003: **Catapult, Cobra, Dunlop, Dynacraf**
Henry-Griffitts, KZG, Lynx, MacGregor, Mizuno, Nickent, Nicklaus, Palme
Perfect, PRGR, Ram, Royal Collection, Snake Eyes, Srixon, Swing Syn
Tommy Armour, Wilson.

TaylorMade wins over **Callaway** in fairway woods usage on th
2003 Nationwide Tour. **Ping** ranks second in victories.

Nationwide Tour - Fairway Woods by Model
Overall vs. Winners

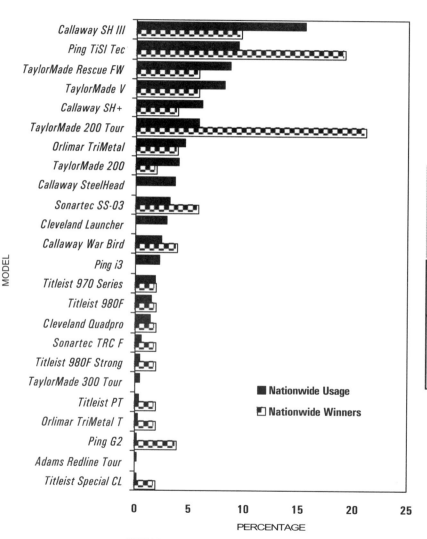

All 2003 Nationwide Tournaments. Sample size: 7,017 fairway woods; 52 winners' fairway woods. Every model used to win a tournament is on this chart.

TaylorMade's 200 Tour model scores themost wins.

FAIRWAY WOODS: PRO USAGE

LPGA Tour - Fairway Woods by Brand
Overall vs. Winners

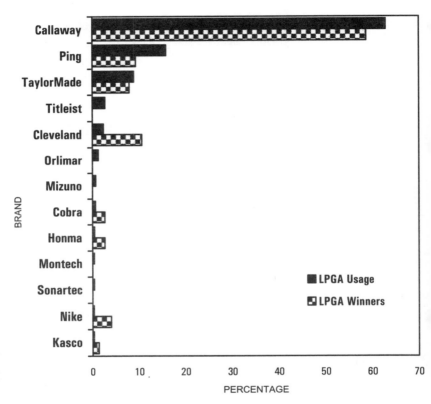

All 2003 LPGA Tournaments. Sample size: 11,281 fairway woods; 75 winners' fairway woods.

All other fairway wood brands used on LPGA Tour in 2003: **Adams, Bridgestone, Daiwa, Golf Dynamic, Integra, Katana, KZG, Lopez, M Golf, Makser, Montech, PRGR, Ram, S Yard, Sonartec, Srixon.**

Callaway dominates fairway woods on the LPGA Tour, contributing to 60% of all 2003 wins.

Given the high number of fairway woods LPGA players keep in their bag *(see page 124)*, this graph represents more clubs than on any other tour. Ping is ranked #2 among LPGA fairway woods.

FAIRWAY WOODS: PRO USAGE

LPGA Tour - Fairway Woods by Model
Overall vs. Winners

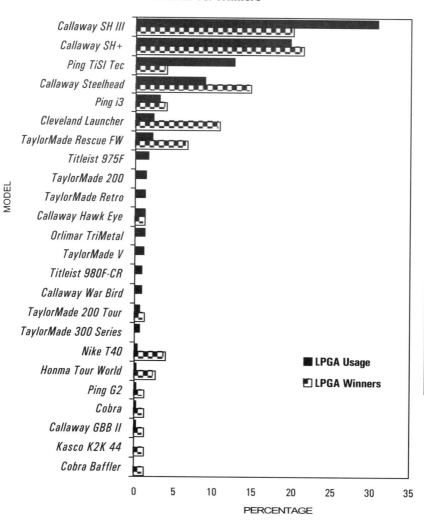

All 2003 LPGA Tournaments.
Sample size: 11,281 fairway woods; 75 winners' fairway woods.
Every model used to win a tournament is on this chart.

Callaway Steelheads are the most popular fairway wood models on
the LPGA Tour in 2003. Ping's TiSI Tec comes in third

FAIRWAY WOODS: PRO USAGE

Japan Tour - Fairway Woods by Brand
Overall vs. Winners

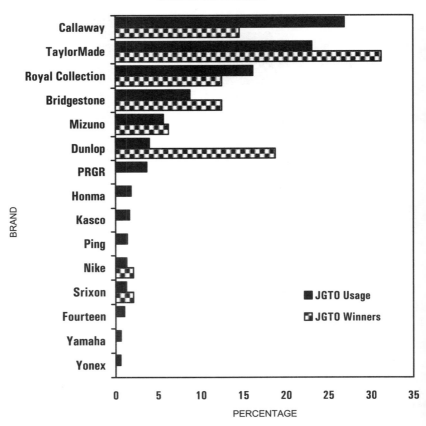

All 2003 JGTO Tournaments.
Sample size: 6,497 fairway woods; 48 winners' fairway woods.

All other fairway wood brands used on JGTO Tour in 2003: **Cleveland, Concept, Daiwa, Gauge Design, Justick, Onoff, Orlimar, Titleist, Tsuruya.**

Callaway fairway woods lead the Japan Golf Tour in usage, while TaylorMade has the most victories.

Japanese Dunlop fairway wood models *(see opposite page)* are not the same as the Dunlop clubs commonly sold in the U.S.

Sonartec is the U.S. name of the Japanese brand Royal Collection.

FAIRWAY WOODS: PRO USAGE

Japan Tour - Fairway Woods by Model
Overall vs. Winners

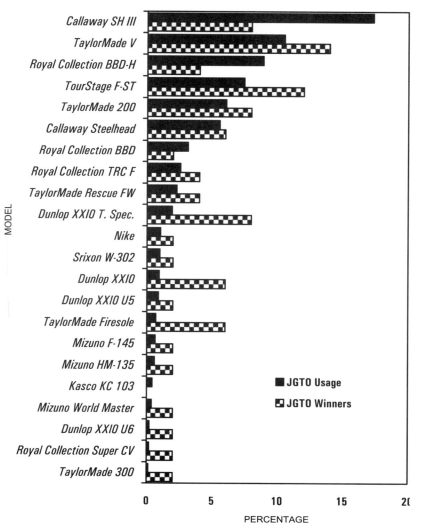

All 2003 JGTO Tournaments.
Sample size: 6,550 fairway woods; 50 winners' fairway woods.
Every model used to win a tournament is on this chart.

The TourStage brand is manufactured by Bridgestone Sports Co, Ltd.

FAIRWAY WOODS:

Tour - Fairway Wood Shafts by Brand
(Graphite & Steel)

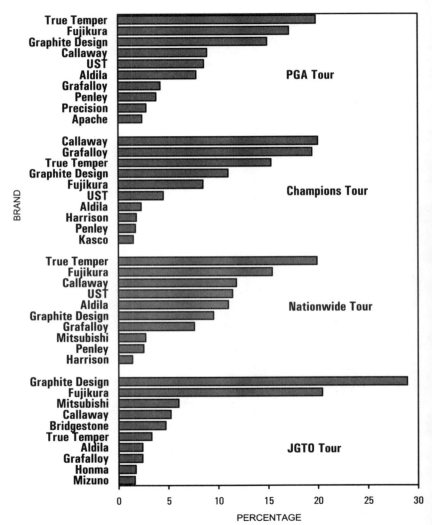

2003 Data. Sample sizes: PGA 10,479 players; Champions 1,149; Nationwide 1,289 ; JGTO 6,550. (JGTO does not have steel detailed models.)

Pros use a wide range of shaft brands and models with their fairway woods. TrueTemper Dynamic Gold shafts are steel.

Tour - Fairway Wood Shafts by Model
(Graphite & Steel)

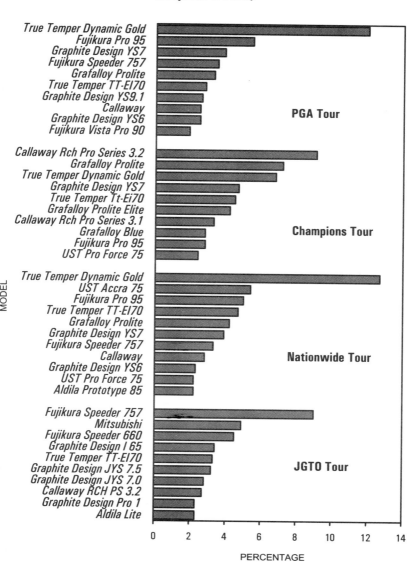

PERCENTAGE

2003 Data. Sample sizes: PGA 10.479 players;
Champions 1,149; Nationwide 1,289; JGTO 6,550.
JGTO data does not include steel models.

FAIRWAY WOODS:

Tour - Fairway Wood Grips by Brand

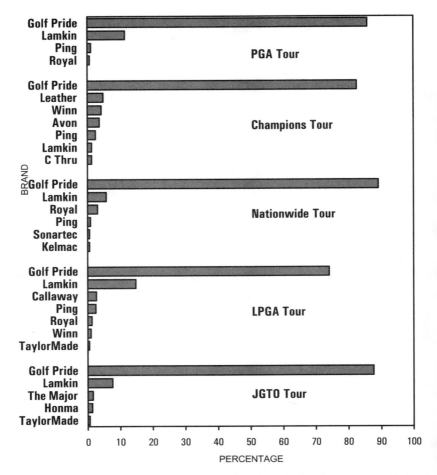

Descending order of leading brand usage for each tour. Leather grips are not surveyed by brand. 2003 data, selected events.

Golf Pride grips are far and away the pros' choice for fairway woods.

The model analysis, *opposite*, breaks out cord and non-cord varities. While G.P. Tour Velvet predominates, the pros also have a preference for Tour Wrap and Victory, in regular and cord.

FAIRWAY WOODS:

Tour - Fairway Wood Grips by Model

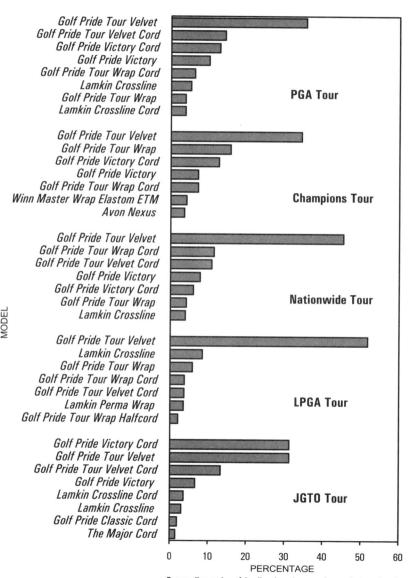

Descending order of leading brand usage for each tour. Leather grips are not surveyed by brand. 2003 data, selected events.

PUTTERS

Chapter 6

Big-headed putters, often referred to as **mallet putters**, continued to gain in popularity. The Odyssey 2-Ball, Titleist Futura, Bettinardi mallets from Ben Hogan, and Bobby Grace models from MacGregor were among the big-headed putters that attracted some prominent converts on the PGA Tour and LPGA Tour.

Odyssey
White Hot 2-Ball

Jim Furyk won his first major, the U.S. Open, with a mallet. **Annika Sorenstam** took two women's majors with a mallet.

Vijay Singh, the leading money winner on the PGA Tour, credited **better putting** for an extraordinary season in which he was able to take the money crown away from Tiger Woods. Vijay's arsenal included a variety of models from three of the top putter designers working today, **Bobby Grace**, **Scotty Cameron** and **Bob Bettinardi**.

Golfers across the United States had the same impulse as Vijay this year: **more than 25% of consumers** surveyed were playing with a **new putter**, the highest ratio of new putters ever recorded since the begin-

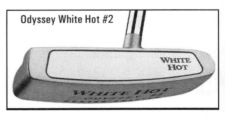

Odyssey White Hot #2

ning of the DARRELL CONSUMER SURVEY in 1981. Clearly, the design innovations spurred by the introduction of the Odyssey 2-ball in 2001 have created new excitement about putters.

Top new consumer models also include the Titleist Scotty Cameron Futura and Studio Design, Odyssey White Hot #2, TaylorMade Rossa Monza and Never Compromise TDP *(see page 157)*.

This year's ALMANAC shows consumer new versus total usage for the first time. As seen on page 156, **Ping**, with its huge installed base of classic putters, ranks high in **total usage** (percentage of all putters in use), while **Odyssey** dominates **new usage** (putters purchased within the past year).

PUTTERS: OVERVIEW

Titleist
Futura

An assortment of **Titleist** models leads in GOLFER SATISFACTION RATINGS *(page 165)*. The STX putter gains the highest marks for overall satisfaction, with Odyssey's TriHot model also touted.

The pros on the **PGA** and **Nationwide Tours** stick with their preferred brand: **Titleist**. Scotty Cameron putters accounted for more than 60% of the wins on the PGA Tour this year *(pages 170-171)*, though a significant portion of the Camerons are custom "prototypes" created specifically for individual players.

LPGA, Champions and **Japan Golf Tour** pros picked **Odyssey** more than any other putter this year, with the 2-ball the leading model on each tour.

Other putters popular on the pro tours include Ping, TaylorMade, Never Compromise, Kevin Burns, See More, and Gauge Design *(pages 171 to 179)*.

In PGA PERFORMANCE STATISTICS, both Titleist and Odyssey averaged an identical 1.796 putts per hole. The lesser-known STX brand scored best on this measure—but shaved only 3/100ths of a putt off the average *(pages 182-187)*.

For their putter **grips**, the pros have a special affinity for **Winn**, which leads on the Champions and LPGA Tours. Other popular grips include Titleist and Odyssey stock grips, as well as Lamkin and Golf Pride *(pages 180-181)*.

Titleist
Scotty Cameron Newport

Ping G2

Odyssey TriHot

Never Compromise TDP

Putters

Consumer Putter Usage by Brand

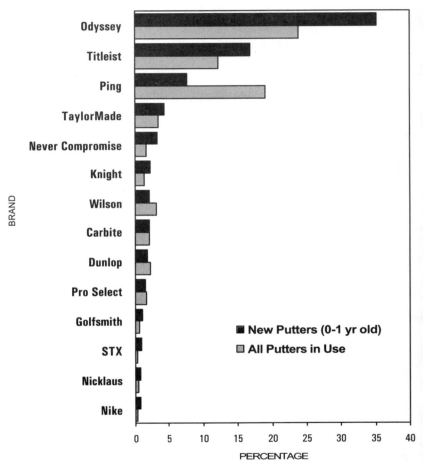

Black bars show brand share of new (less than 1 year old) equipment in use.
Gray bars show percentage of all consumer equipment in use. Nationwide
on-course consumer survey conducted summer 2003; 3,241 respondents.

Odyssey leads in **new consumer putters**, shown in **black**, while Ping
is second in usage of **all putters**, new and old, shown in **gray**.

More than 20% of the new putters in our nationwide survey were
Odyssey 2-Ball models *(see opposite page)*. This model is the favorite
among all handicaps and age groups *(see pp. 158-9.)*

Consumer Putter Usage by Model

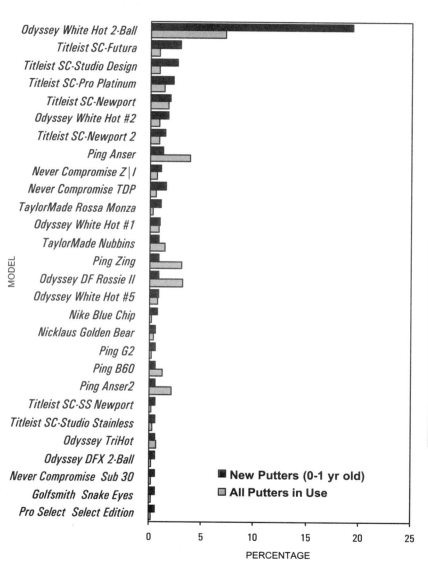

Percentage share of consumer equipment in use. Nationwide on-course consumer survey conducted summer 2003; 3,241 respondents.

PUTTERS: WHAT CONSUMERS USE MOST

Putter Model Usage by Handicap

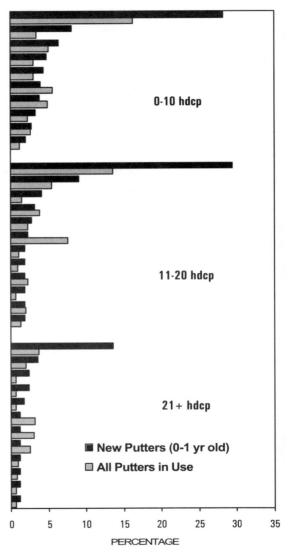

Percentage share of consumer equipment in use. Nationwide on-course consumer survey conducted summer 2003; 794 respondents for "New Putters" and 3,137 respondents for "All Putters in Use".

PUTTERS: WHAT CONSUMERS USE MOST

Putter Model Usage by Age

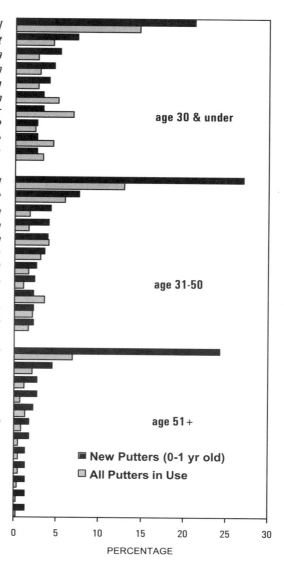

Percentage share of consumer equipment in use. Nationwide on-course consumer survey conducted summer 2002; 3,031 respondents.

Darrell Golfer Satisfaction Ratings™
Putter Brands by Handicap

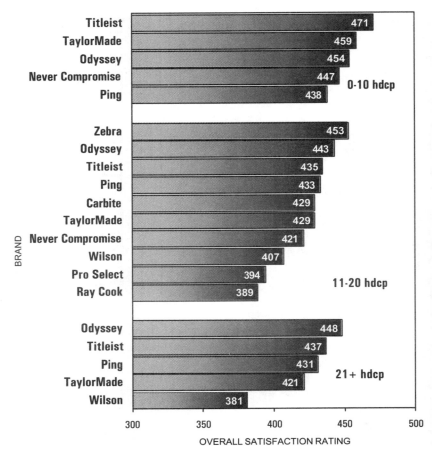

"How satisfied are you with your equipment?" 500 is most satisfied. 100 is least satisfied. Consumer golfers rate the equipment they are actually using the day of the survey. 2,265 opinion respondents. (Minimum of 15 responses per subgroup for brands shown.)

Consumer opinions rank a variety of Odyssey, Titleist and Ping putter models at the highest overall satisfaction ratings.

As noted in other chapters, more-skilled golfers generally give their equipment higher scores.

Darrell Golfer Satisfaction Ratings™
Putter Models by Handicap

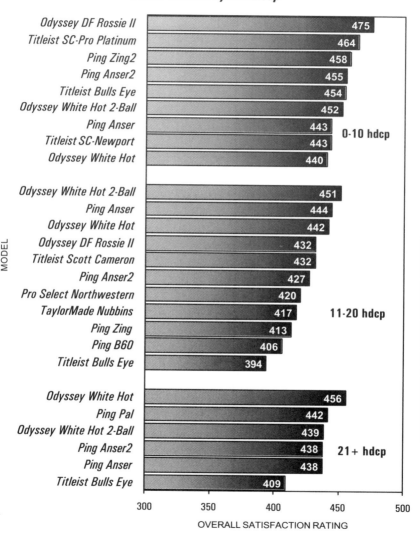

"How satisfied are you with your equipment?" 500 is most satisfied. 100 is least satisfied. Consumer golfers rate the equipment they are actually using the day of the survey. 2,265 opinion respondents. (Minimum of 12 responses per subgroup for brands/models shown.)

PUTTERS: CONSUMER OPINIONS

Darrell Golfer Satisfaction Ratings™
Putter Brands by Age

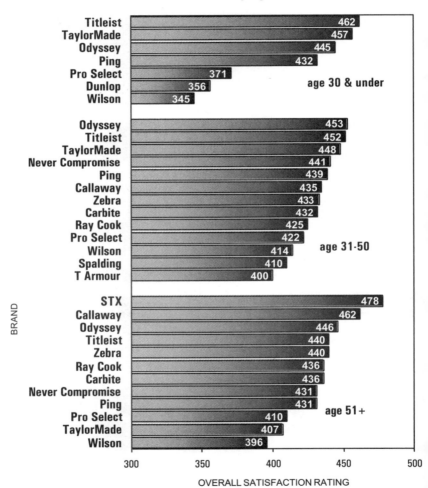

OVERALL SATISFACTION RATING

"How satisfied are you with your equipment?" 500 is most satisfied. 100 is least satisfied. Consumer golfers rate the equipment they are actually using the day of the survey. 2,265 opinion respondents. (Minimum of 15 responses per subgroup for brands shown.)

Putter satisfaction ratings by age do not correlate with the satisfaction ratings by handicap. (*Compare the models shown on p. 161 with those on p. 163.*) Opinions about putter models are peculiar to the user.

Darrell Golfer Satisfaction Ratings™
Putter Models by Age

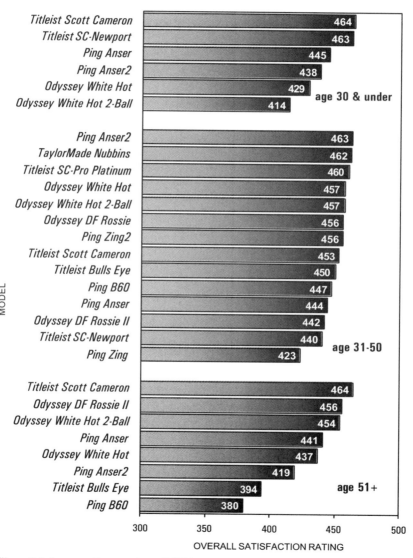

"How satisfied are you with your equipment?" 500 is most satisfied. 100 is least satisfied. Consumer golfers rate the equipment they are actually using the day of the survey. 2,265 opinion respondents. (Minimum of 12 responses per subgroup for models shown.)

Darrell Golfer Satisfaction Ratings™
Putter Brands by Feature

—— Satisfaction SCORE by Equipment Feature ——

PUTTERS

(Listed Alphabetically)	Overall	Feel	Value	Appearance	Accuracy	Forgiveness
Average Score	431	437	431	427	431	427
Callaway	*448*	439	*442*	*439*	*453*	*445*
Carbite	433	437	*440*	421	435	430
Component	389	394	394	406	394	378
Dunlop	381	394	409	376	379	376
Knight	383	394	389	383	389	383
Mizuno	432	442	421	*453*	426	421
Never Compromise	434	441	432	430	439	432
Odyssey	*449*	*456*	436	*447*	*450*	*447*
Ping	434	436	436	433	*435*	430
Pro Select	400	396	407	375	404	404
Ray Cook	411	414	417	406	400	403
Spalding	405	410	425	395	415	405
STX	*472*	*461*	*467*	*472*	*472*	*461*
T Armour	410	*455*	425	390	405	410
TaylorMade	433	440	425	417	427	424
Titleist	*451*	*461*	*446*	*451*	*453*	*444*
Wilson	394	400	410	388	396	394
Zebra	*444*	*444*	*447*	431	439	*439*

"How satisfied are you with your equipment?" 500 is most satisfied. 100 is least satisfied. Consumer golfers rate the equipment they are actually using the day of the survey. 2,265 opinion respondents. (Minimum of 15 responses per subgroup for brands shown.)

❖ Compare each score to the average seen in the top row.

❖ Numbers in ***bold italic*** indicate top 5 scores in each category.

❖ Scores for individual models are listed on the opposite page.

Consumers' most highly rated putters brands are **Titleist, Odyssey**... and a lesser-known name, **STX**.

Several Titleist Scotty Cameron varieties receive high scores across the board, as seen on the opposite page.

See page 11 for more information on Golfer Satisfaction Ratings.

PUTTERS: CONSUMER OPINIONS

Darrell Golfer Satisfaction Ratings™
Putter Models by Feature

—— Satisfaction SCORE by Equipment Feature ——

PUTTERS (Listed Alphabetically)	Overall	Feel	Value	Appearance	Accuracy	Forgivene
Average Score	*431*	*437*	*431*	*427*	*431*	*427*
Callaway Bobby Jones	440	427	440	427	450	433
Mizuno TPM	432	442	421	453	426	421
Never Compromise Z|I	447	453	*447*	433	440	433
Odyssey DF Rossie	451	453	439	442	453	453
Odyssey DF Rossie II	453	457	440	442	456	454
Odyssey TriHot	*471*	*488*	441	*471*	*471*	*482*
Odyssey White Hot 1	453	453	433	453	453	447
Odyssey White Hot 2-Ball	450	457	428	442	452	449
Ping Anser	443	445	*451*	446	443	446
Ping Anser2	438	443	443	435	446	433
Ping B60	423	419	414	419	419	414
Ping Pal	435	435	443	426	452	427
Ping Zing	430	437	434	427	432	427
Ping Zing2	448	456	*448*	441	456	448
Pro SelectNorthwestern	419	419	425	387	425	425
Ray Cook	411	414	417	406	400	403
STX	*472*	*461*	*467*	*472*	*472*	*461*
T Armour	410	455	425	390	405	410
TaylorMade	433	440	425	417	427	424
TaylorMade Nubbins	432	436	429	436	418	425
TaylorMade Rossa	437	437	384	405	426	426
Titleist SC-Futura	*471*	*488*	*447*	*471*	*476*	*471*
Titleist SC-Newport	*458*	*467*	*462*	*462*	*467*	*458*
Titleist SC-Pro Platinum	*470*	*470*	443	*487*	*487*	*461*
Zebra	444	444	*447*	431	439	439

"How satisfied are you with your equipment?" 500 is most satisfied. 100 is least satisfied. Numbers in **bold italic** *indicate top 5 scores for each category. Consumer golfers rate the equipment they are actually using the day of the survey. 2,265 opinion respondents. (Minimum of 10 responses per subgroup for models shown.)*

Satisfaction scores for the most common putters, listed above, may not correlate directly to the brand scores on the opposite page, which are an average of that brand's models in use.

Putters

Consumer Opinions

Puttering Around

(From top to bottom) Yes C-Groove, Bettinardi, Ben Hogan by Bettinardi,
TaylorMade Rossa Monza, MacGregor by Bobby Grace & Ping Anser

Top Putter Models
At Major Amateur Tournaments

U.S. AMATEUR
Odyssey White Hot 2-Ball
Titleist SC-Newport 2
Ping Anser 2
Titleist SC -Newport
Titleist SC -Newport Mil-Spec
Titleist SC -Newport 2.5
Odyssey DFX 2-Ball

Us WOMEN'S
Odyssey White Hot 2-Ball
Titleist SC-Newport 2
Titleist SC-Newport Midslant
Titleist SC-Newport Mil-Spec
Odyssey 1100 DFX
Odyssey Rossie 2
Odyssey White Hot 2

NCAA DIV 1 MEN'S
Odyssey White Hot 2-Ball
Titleist SC-Newport Stainless
Odyssey Tri Hot 3
Titleist SC-Newport 2
Odyssey White Hot 5
Titleist SC-Newport
Odyssey DFX 2-Ball

NCAA WOMENS
Odyssey White Hot 2-Ball
Odyssey White Hot 5
Odyssey Tri Hot 3
Odyssey White Hot 1
Odyssey Tri Hot 1
Odyssey Tri Hot 2
Odyssey White Hot 2

U.S. BOYS JUNIOR
Odyssey White Hot 2-Ball
Titleist SC-Newport 2
Titleist SC-Newport Mil-Spec
Titleist SC-Newport Midslant
Titleist SC-Newport
Titleist SC-Prototype
Titleist SC-Newport 2.5
Titleist SC-Futura

U.S. GIRLS JUNIOR
Odyssey White Hot 2-Ball
Odyssey White Hot 5
Odyssey Tri Hot 3
Odyssey White Hot 1
Odyssey Tri Hot 1
Odyssey Tri Hot 2
Odyssey White Hot 2
Ping Anser 2

2003 Data.

Odyssey and Titleist blanket the list of top putter models in use at major amateur events.

So Many to Choose From

(From top to bottom) Never Compromise Sub30, Odyssey DFX, STX Sync Tour,
Odyssey White Hot Rossie, Mizuno & Never Comnpromise

Tour - Putters by Brand

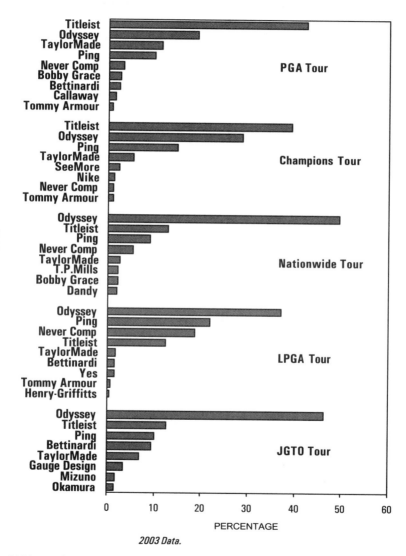

2003 Data.

In 2003, Titleist brand putters are most used on the PGA and Champions Tours, while Odyssey leads on the Nationwide, LPGA and Japan Golf Tours.

PGA Tour - Putters by Brand
Overall vs. Winners

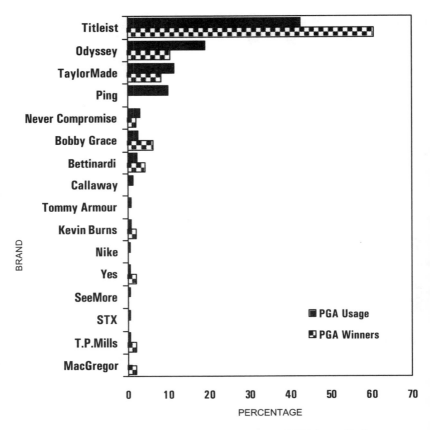

All 2003 PGA Tournaments. Sample size: 6,504 players; 48 winners.

*All other putter brands used on PGA Tour in 2003: **Adams, Artemis, Bridgestone, Carbite, Cleveland, Daiwa, Dandy, Dogleg Right, Drosso, Dunlop, Farrar, Fisher Touch, Fox, Gauge Design, Guerin Rife, H. Matsumoto, Kirk Currie, Lynx, Macgregor, Mizuno, Nicklaus, P2 Solution, Pendulum, Precis, Pure Stroke, Rick Hamilton, Solo, T.Moore, Teardrop, Top-Flite, Wilson, Zen Oracle.***

Titleist putters dominate the PGA Tour. Note the many different Scotty Cameron putter models, including the "Tiger" *(see opposite page.)*

TaylorMade joins the top ranks to third place in 2003.

PGA Tour - Putters by Model
Overall vs. Winners

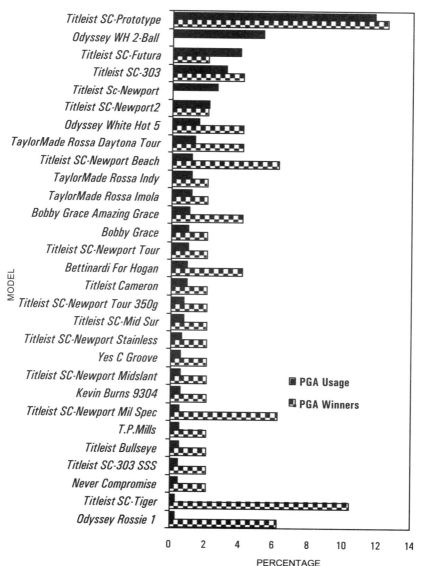

All 2003 PGA Tournaments. Sample size: 6,504 players; 48 winners.
Every model used to win a tournament is on this chart.

Champions Tour - Putters by Brand
Overall vs. Winners

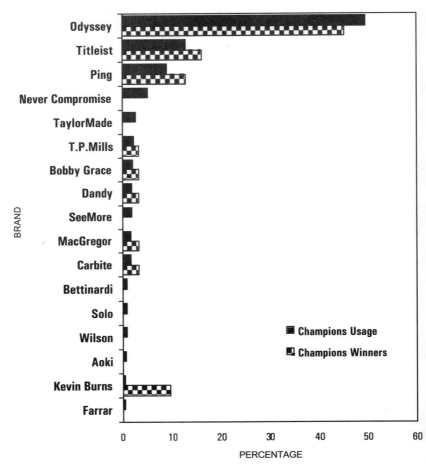

All 2003 Champions Tournaments. Sample size: 2,608 players; 31 winners.

All other putter brands used on Champions Tour in 2003: **Brazos, Bristol, Callaway, Clay Long, Cleveland, Closar, Closar, Cobra, Dogleg Right, Fisher Touch, Gauge Design, Golf Ventures, H. Matsumoto, John Byron, Langert, Leading Edge, Maltby, Mizuno, Nicklaus, Old Master, Otey Crisman, Palmer, Pelz, Perfect Putter, Player, Pole Kat, Pure Stroke, Rainbow, Ram, Ray Cook, Regal, Slazenger, Slotline, Snowdon, Stx, Teardrop, Tommy Armour, Top Flite, Trueline, Yes.**

Champions Tour players use Odyssey putters more than any other brand. The Odyssey 2-Ball is the putter of Champions *(see opposite)*.

Champions Tour - Putters by Model
Overall vs. Winners

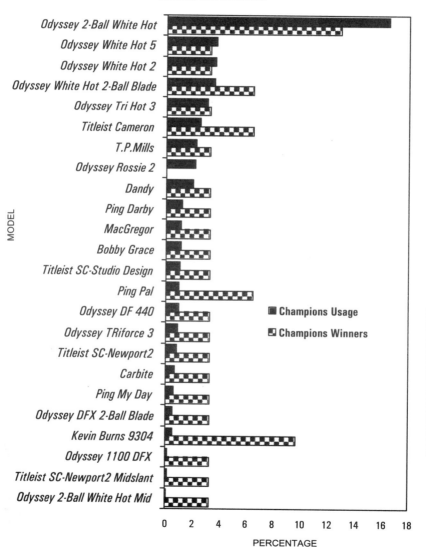

All 2003 Champions Tournaments.
Sample size: 6,608 players; 31 winners.
Every model used to win a tournament is on this chart.

Nationwide Tour - Putters by Brand
Overall vs. Winners

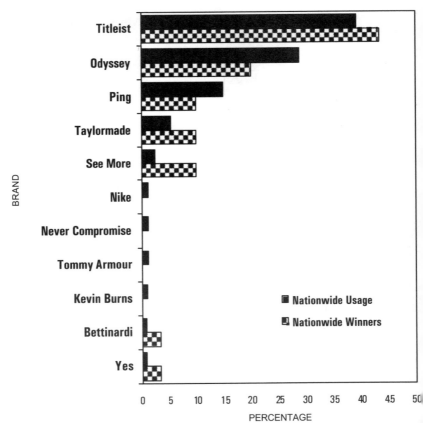

All 2003 Nationwide Tournaments. Sample size: 4,477 players; 30 winners.
All other putter brands used on LPGA Tour in 2003; **Adams, Bobby Grace,**
Bridgestone, Carbite, Clay Long, Cleveland, Copper Stix, Dogleg Right,
Drossos, Dynatech, Guerin Rife, Henry-Griffitts, John Byron, Kirk
Currie, Leading Edge, Linertia, MacGregor, Make Everything, Mizuno,
Nicklaus, Palmer, Pendulum, Penick, Precise, Ray Cook, Slazenger,
Slotline, STX, T.Moore, T.P.Mills, TearDrop, Wilson..

Titleist tops the Nationwide Tour in putter usage and wins.
20 different putter models score wins in 2003 *(see opposite page).*

The top putter models on the Nationwide Tour differ from those on
the PGA Tour *(see p. 171.)*

Nationwide Tour - Putters by Model
Overall vs. Winners

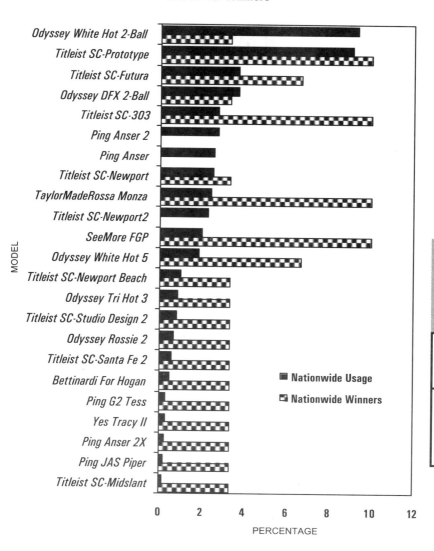

All 2003 Nationwide Tournaments. Sample size: 4,447 players;
30 winners. Every model used to win a tournament is on this chart.

LPGA Tour - Putters by Brand
Overall vs. Winners

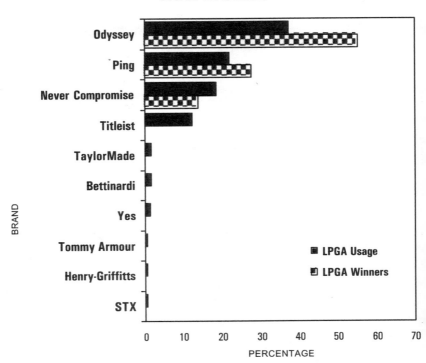

All 2003 LPGA Tournaments. Sample size: 3,857 players; 29 winners.

*All other putter brands used on LPGA Tour in 2003: **Bobby Grace,
Carbite, Dave Hicks, Honma, Infiniti, John Byron, Kirk Currie,
Mizuno, Nicklaus, Positive, Ray Cook, SeeMore, Slazenger,
Sportsman, Srixon, T.P.Mills, TearDrop, Wilson.***

The three leading putter brands are responsible for all wins on the
LPGA Tour in 2003: **Odyssey**, **Ping** and **Never Compromise**.

Odyssey's 2-Ball Series putters claim the top two models in use.
(See chart opposite.) 18 different putter models scored victories during
the season.

LPGA Tour - Putters by Model
Overall vs. Winners

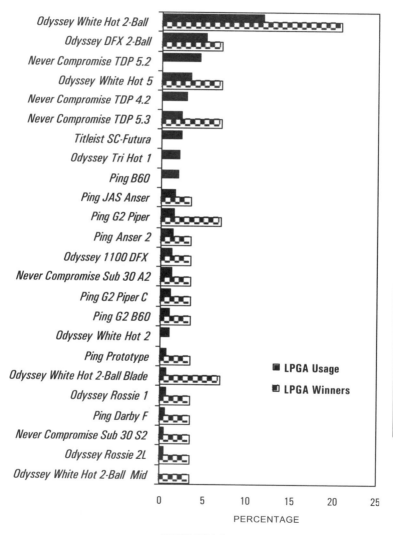

All 2003 LPGA Tournaments. Sample size: 3,857 players;
29 winners.

Japan Tour - Putters by Brand
Overall vs. Winners

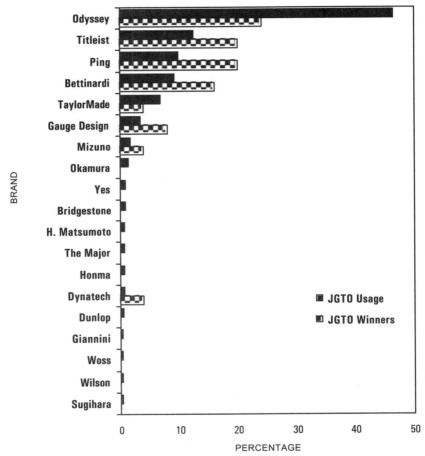

All 2003 JGTO Tournaments. Sample size: 3,341 players; 25 winners.

All other putter brands used on JGTO Tour in 2003: Aoki, Bobby Grace, Carbite, Cobra, Grand Prix, John Byron, Kevin Burns, MacGregor, Never Compromise, Srixon, STX, TearDrop ,Tommy Armour , Tad.Moore.

While Odyssey putters lead in overall JGTO usage, Titleist, Ping and Bettinardi putters are competitive in victories in 2003.

Some leading Japanese putter brands may be unfamiliar to US readers: H. Matsumoto, The Major, Woss and Sugihara.

Japan Tour - Putters by Model
Overall vs. Winners

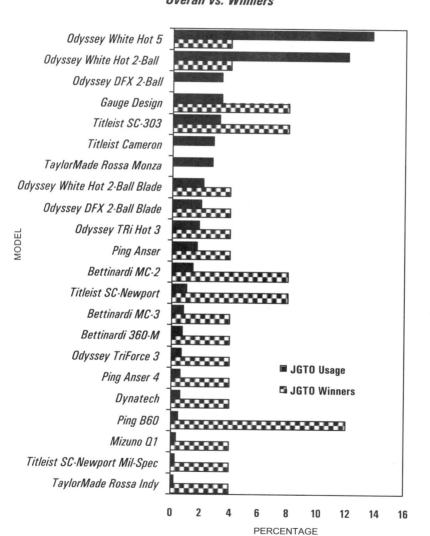

All 2003 JGTO Tournaments. Sample size: 3,341 players;
25 winners. Every model used to win a tournament is on this chart.

Ping's B-60 model putter captures the most wins on the Japan Golf
Tour in 2003.

Tour - Putter Grips by Brand

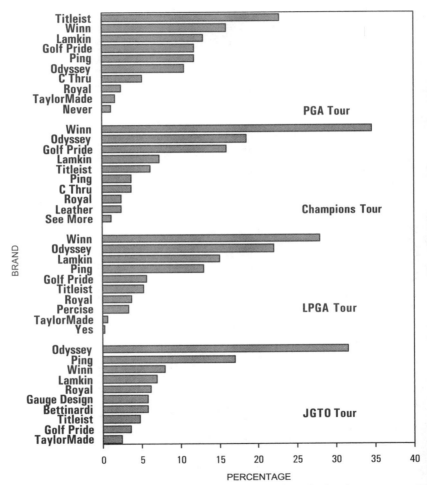

Descending order of leading brand usage for each tour. Leather grips are not surveyed by brand. 2003 data, selected events.

The **Winn** brand is a popular choice for pro putter grips.

Because the putter brand now appears on many grips, Titleist, Odyssey and Ping are among the leading names in this analysis.

Compare with driver grip models *(see p. 114.)*

Tour - Putter Grips by Model

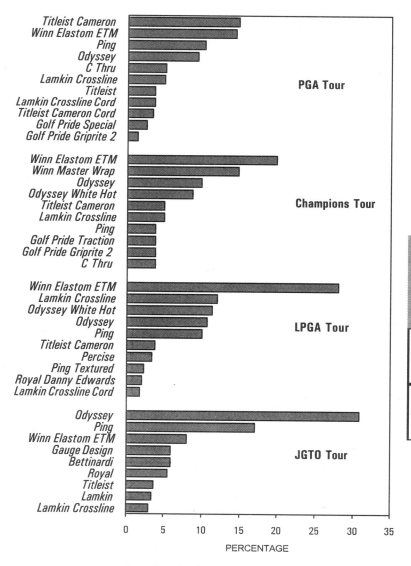

Descending order of leading model usage for each tour. Leather grips are not surveyed by model. 2003 data, selected events.

2003 PGA Tour Putter Statistics
For Major Brands and Models

Putter Brand and Model	# of Uses	Sum of Official Money $	Average Winnings per Use $	Average G.I.R. Putts per Hole*
BETTINARDI				
FOR HOGAN	62	3,994,779.00	67,708.12	1.789
TOUR ONLY	24	362,382.00	15,099.25	1.747
360-XM	10	325,636.00	40,704.50	1.830
TOUR EXEMPT	11	105,077.00	9,552.45	1.818
Sum/Average of All Models	157	6,332,821.00	42,789.33	1.793
BOBBY GRACE				
AMAZING GRACE	68	3,770,962.00	57,135.79	1.791
FAT LADY	25	344,494.00	13,779.76	1.769
Sum/Average of All Models	159	8,616,781.00	55,953.12	1.784
BRIDGESTONE				
K.BURNS TOURSTAGE	15	66,105.00	4,407.00	1.798
Sum/Average of All Models	15	66,105.00	4,407.00	1.798
CALLAWAY				
TT 1	33	855,773.00	25,932.52	1.784
TITUN	13	502,281.00	41,856.75	1.735
TT 2	10	230,295.00	23,029.50	1.866
Sum/Average of All Models	89	2,506,591.00	28,483.99	1.794
DROSSOS				
Sum/Average of All Models	12	19,155.00	1,596.25	1.818
DUNLOP				
Sum/Average of All Models	12	19,155.00	1,596.25	1.818
FOX				
Sum/Average of All Models	13	142,796.00	10,984.31	1.847
GAUGE DESIGN				
Sum/Average of All Models	10	242,173.00	20,881.10	1.778
GUERIN RIFE				
Sum/Average of All Models	18	238,200.00	14,887.50	1.813

*Average G.I.R. Putts Per Hole is derived from the PGA "Total Greens in Regulation" and "Total Greens in Regulation Putts" statistics. (G.I.R. putts are divided by the number of greens hit in regulation, eliminating the effect of chipping close and one-putting.)
Cut players' putting statistics are included in the above averages.

2003 PGA Tour Putter Statistics
For Major Brands and Models

Putter Brand and Model	# of Uses	Sum of Official Money $	Average Winnings per Use $	Average G.I.R. Putts per Hole*
KEVIN BURNS				
9304	38	1,315,485.00	36,541.25	1.801
Sum/Average of All Models	55	1,633,865.00	30,827.64	1.808
MACGREGOR				
BOBBY GRACE	12	859,738.00	78,158.00	1.783
Sum/Average of All Models	12	859,738.00	78,158.00	1.783
MIZUNO				
Sum/Average of All Models	11	8,820.00	801.82	1.837
NEVER COMPROMISE				
SUB30M3	34	1,851,176.00	54,446.35	1.745
TDP 2.2	26	1,335,736.00	58,075.48	1.813
ZI ALPHA	18	473,181.00	26,287.83	1.781
TDP 4.2	22	453,226.00	20,601.18	1.775
PROTOTYPE	12	297,048.00	24,754.00	1.784
VOODO	16	127,701.00	7,981.31	1.848
SUB30A2	13	56,211.00	4,323.92	1.837
Sum/Average of All Models	201	7,059,387.00	35,834.45	1.795
NIKE				
SPIKE	30	334,763.00	11,543.55	1.820
PROTOTYPE	13	120,259.00	10,021.58	1.779
Sum/Average of All Models	46	518,022.00	12,047.02	1.812
ODYSSEY				
2-BALL WH	346	9,531,549.00	28,033.97	1.802
WHITE HOT 5	103	5,667,697.00	55,565.66	1.773
ROSSIE 1	18	3,737,956.00	207,664.22	1.797
ROSSIE 2	78	3,037,923.00	38,947.73	1.774
WHITE HOT 4	22	1,817,243.00	82,601.95	1.804
DFX 2-BALL	112	1,465,458.00	13,322.35	1.820
WHITE HOT LONG	17	1,116,015.00	65,647.94	1.789
TRI HOT 3	103	1,046,188.00	10,256.75	1.799

Putters

Tour Stats

Minimum 10 uses per season. Averages are less reliable for models with fewer than 50 uses.

2003 PGA Tour Putter Statistics
For Major Brands and Models

Putter Brand and Model	# of Uses	Sum of Official Money $	Average Winnings per Use $	Average G.I.R. Putts per Hole*
ODYSSEY				
6600 DFX	37	972,286.00	27,007.94	1.780
TRI HOT 2	17	895,665.00	52,686.18	1.834
DF 330	39	825,753.00	21,730.34	1.770
WHITE HOT 2	39	810,611.00	21,331.87	1.781
5500 DFX	13	621,779.00	47,829.15	1.718
TRIFORCE 2	16	550,436.00	34,402.25	1.783
WHITE HOT 6	14	484,176.00	34,584.00	1.806
TRI HOT 1	30	455,530.00	15,184.33	1.791
WH 2-BALL BLADE	22	449,683.00	21,413.48	1.844
3300 DFX	17	255,884.00	15,052.00	1.738
WHITE HOT 1	27	236,317.00	9,089.12	1.817
TRIFORCE 3	29	235,517.00	8,121.28	1.787
DF 440	10	232,646.00	23,264.60	1.795
DF 334	19	208,073.00	12,239.59	1.777
WHITE HOT MID	17	200,904.00	11,817.88	1.816
9900 DFX	11	180,583.00	16,416.64	1.847
DF 550	20	150,590.00	7,529.50	1.784
DFX 2-BALL BLADE	12	52,693.00	4,391.08	1.791
Sum/Average of All Models	1242	35,859,058.00	29,296.62	1.796
PENDULUM				
Sum/Average of All Models	11	791,565.00	71,960.45	1.803
PING				
ANSER	103	5,602,840.00	55,473.66	1.778
JAS ANSER	113	2,730,841.00	25,521.88	1.795
ANSER F	29	2,350,630.00	83,951.07	1.771
ANSER 2	74	2,192,456.00	30,450.78	1.799
ZING 2	71	1,796,549.00	25,664.99	1.789
ZING PROTO	22	1,120,025.00	53,334.52	1.787
PAL 4	27	786,912.00	29,144.89	1.799

Minimum 10 uses per season. Averages are less reliable for models with fewer than 50 uses.

2003 PGA Tour Putter Statistics
For Major Brands and Models

Putter Brand and Model	# of Uses	Sum of Official Money $	Average Winnings per Use $	Average G.I.R. Putts per Hole*
PING				
G2	14	619,503.00	44,250.21	1.765
G2 C10	13	419,658.00	32,281.38	1.812
G2 ANSER B	18	399,777.00	22,209.83	1.833
PROTOTYPE	19	380,343.00	20,018.05	1.809
J BLADE	14	259,546.00	18,539.00	1.799
C67	12	244,834.00	20,402.83	1.797
ANSER TI3	10	232,093.00	23,209.30	1.771
B60	10	156,254.00	15,625.40	1.866
Sum/Average of All Models	640	20,885,852.00	33,363.98	1.797
SEE MORE				
FGP	34	1,775,554.00	53,804.67	1.790
Sum/Average of All Models	43	2,251,721.00	56,293.03	1.819
STX				
STX	32	1,452,320.00	45,385.00	1.751
Sum/Average of All Models	41	2,141,866.00	52,240.63	1.767
T.P.MILLS				
T.P.Mills	36	1,200,568.00	35,310.82	1.791
Sum/Average of All Models	38	1,253,568.00	34,821.33	1.787
TAYLORMADE				
ROSSA MONZA	138	3,993,675.00	29,582.78	1.801
ROSSA IMOLA	75	3,988,311.00	54,634.40	1.772
ROSSA DAYTONA TOUR	89	3,248,837.00	36,918.60	1.811
ROSSA INDY	77	3,015,271.00	40,203.61	1.807
ROSSA MARANELLO	42	1,148,219.00	28,005.34	1.801
ROSSA DAYTONA	68	860,772.00	12,847.34	1.794
ROSSA SEBRING	32	712,164.00	22,255.13	1.797
ROSSA DAYTONA SPORT	36	694,612.00	19,846.06	1.812
TPA 8	13	459,091.00	35,314.69	1.767
ROSSA FONTANA	41	395,972.00	9,657.85	1.827

Putters

Tour

Stats

Minimum 10 uses per season. Averages are less reliable for models with fewer than 50 uses.

2003 PGA Tour Putter Statistics
For Major Brands and Models

Putter Brand and Model	# of Uses	Sum of Official Money $	Average Winnings per Use $	Average G.I.R. Putts per Hole*
TAYLORMADE				
ROSSA PROTOTYPE	13	395,076.00	32,923.00	1.750
ROSSA MODINA	29	374,403.00	13,371.54	1.839
ROSSA LAMBEAU	20	306,062.00	15,303.10	1.800
ROSSA LONG BEACH	19	220,118.00	12,228.78	1.843
ROSSA INDY SPORT	10	18,902.00	1,890.20	1.775
Sum/Average of All Models	740	20,693,073.00	28,542.17	1.802
TEARDROP				
Sum/Average of All Models	11	1,095,850.00	99,622.73	1.768
TITLEIST				
SC-PROTOTYPE	765	25,628,249.00	34,820.99	1.797
SC-FUTURA	257	8,607,311.00	34,567.51	1.785
SC-303	206	7,183,822.00	35,563.48	1.804
SC-TIGER	18	6,673,413.00	370,745.17	1.732
SC-NEWPORT BEACH	78	6,069,514.00	78,824.86	1.791
SC-NEWPORT MIL SPEC	36	4,972,146.00	138,115.17	1.799
SC-NEWPORT2	139	4,837,732.00	35,571.56	1.793
SC-STUDIO DESIGN	58	3,491,011.00	62,339.48	1.800
SC-NEWPORT	173	3,262,440.00	19,892.93	1.809
SC-NEWPORT MIDSLANT	39	2,733,210.00	73,870.54	1.789
SC-LAGUNA MIDSLANT	29	2,722,406.00	93,876.07	1.755
SC-MID SUR	49	2,615,708.00	55,653.36	1.789
BULLSEYE	35	2,596,416.00	76,365.18	1.811
SC-SANTA FE	62	2,118,378.00	34,727.51	1.801
SC-TOUR	45	2,098,071.00	46,623.80	1.773
CAMERON	61	2,025,250.00	33,754.17	1.780
SC-303 SSS	32	2,005,701.00	64,700.03	1.752
SC-NEWPORT STAINLESS	42	1,882,481.00	44,820.98	1.789
SC-NEWPORT TOUR	64	1,294,122.00	20,541.62	1.812
SC-NEWPORT2.5	37	1,272,585.00	34,394.19	1.809

2003 Season, all PGA tournaments for which statistics are available. Only brands and models with minimum 10 uses are listed above. Overall brand sums and averages, however, do include all models surveyed.

2003 PGA Tour Putter Statistics
For Major Brands and Models

Putter Brand and Model	# of Uses	Sum of Official Money $	Average Winnings per Use $	Average G.I.R. Putts per Hole*
TITLEIST				
SC-NEWPORT 303	30	1,264,561.00	43,605.55	1.803
SC-NEWPORT2 MIDSLANT	15	1,248,797.00	89,199.79	1.779
SC-NEWPORT2 STAIN.	27	1,228,238.00	45,490.30	1.821
SC-NEWPORT TOUR 350G	49	1,045,536.00	21,337.47	1.770
SC-CALIENTE	27	791,107.00	29,300.26	1.761
BULLSEYE SC	25	735,465.00	29,418.60	1.786
SC-STUDIO DESIGN 2	28	555,381.00	19,835.04	1.793
SC-LAGUNA	24	475,800.00	19,825.00	1.833
SC-NEWPORT2 TOUR	41	454,990.00	11,666.41	1.829
SC-DEL MAR 3.5	17	313,285.00	18,428.53	1.778
SC-NAPA	23	272,214.00	11,835.39	1.815
SC-STUDIO STAINLESS	18	267,976.00	14,887.56	1.834
SC-350	21	263,689.00	12,556.62	1.822
SC-DEL MAR	10	228,540.00	28,567.50	1.833
SC-303 GSS	16	208,300.00	13,018.75	1.775
SC-LAGUNA 2.5	24	180,824.00	7,534.33	1.808
SC-STUDIO DESIGN 2.5	14	81,299.00	6,253.77	1.789
SC-STUDIO DESIGN 5	12	45,727.00	3,810.58	1.857
Sum/Average of All Models	2759	105,300,802.00	39,276.69	1.796
TOMMY ARMOUR				
PROTOTYPE	19	910,189.00	47,904.68	1.809
TODD SONES	19	461,509.00	25,639.39	1.791
Sum/Average of All Models	55	1,691,711.00	31,919.08	1.794
WILSON				
8813	11	115,475.00	10,497.73	1.784
8802	10	76,208.00	7,620.80	1.874
Sum/Average of All Models	23	191,683.00	8,334.04	1.845
YES				
C GROOVE	39	3,858,179.00	101,531.03	1.774
Sum/Average of All Models	44	3,998,307.00	92,983.88	1.785

Putters

Tour

Stats

$ = US Dollars. Data is copyrighted by Darrell Survey and may not be used without permission.

GOLF BAGS & TOURNAMENT WINNERS

Chapter 7

A golf bag serves two purposes for both Tour professionals and recreational golfers alike: **carrying equipment**, and **making a statement**.

Thanks to yearly refinements in bag design, carrying equipment has never been more pleasant. **Improved designs**, including high-tech fabrics, improved stands, comfortable straps and an array of pockets have eased the burdens of golfers everywhere.

With regard to making a statement, pros and consumers have slightly different goals. Pros use their bags as **t.v.-camera-friendly billboards** for their primary sponsors, most often the maker of their ball or clubs but also anything from a carmaker to an insurance group — or even a Japanese blue-jean company *(see pages 200 to 206)*.

Consumers are making a statement just for themselves. Will they buy a **TaylorMade** bag to match the new set of rac irons contained within? Or a **Sun Mountain** Superlight bag at only 2.5 pounds? Or the latest **Ping** Hoofer bag to replace their old favorite?

Ping remains tops in total consumer usage of smaller carry bags, while **Callaway** leads in large cart bags *(see page 193)*.

In overall consumer **GOLFER SATISFACTION RATINGS**, the top-rated brands are Cleveland, Sun Mountain, Titleist and TaylorMade *(see page 198)*.

Titleist X48 , TaylormadeTour Stand Bag & Sun Mountain Superlite 3.5 Stand Bags

BAGS: OVERVIEW

Providing another vivid example of the brutal compeition for domination of the pro tours, TaylorMade and Titleist bags tied on the **PGA Tour** this year, with 983 uses each over the course of the season. Titleist bags were number one on the **Champions** and **Nationwide** Tours, while native Bridgestone bags lead on the **Japan Golf Tour**.

Other leading bag brands in pro usage are Cleveland, Nike, Mizuno, Ping, Club Glove and Adams *(see pages 199-204)*.

A pro's bag branded with a clubmaker's name provides a good clue as to what clubs are in the bag. Our list of **tournament winners** and their bag brands *(starting on page 205)* thus provides insight into the brands endorsed and used by winning pros. Cleveland certainly made a splash on the bag of **Vijay Singh**, while **Annika Sörenstam**'s bag bore the Callaway name.

In an interesting sidelight to the **function vs. form** debate, most club-makers have their bags made by bag-only specialists like Sun Mountain, Izzo, Belding Sports, Ogio, Datrek, Burton and Jones.

Ping is the exception, a club company that manufactures its own bags.

Callaway Stand Bag, Cleveland Tour & Ping Cart Bag

Bags

Consumer Bag Usage by Brand

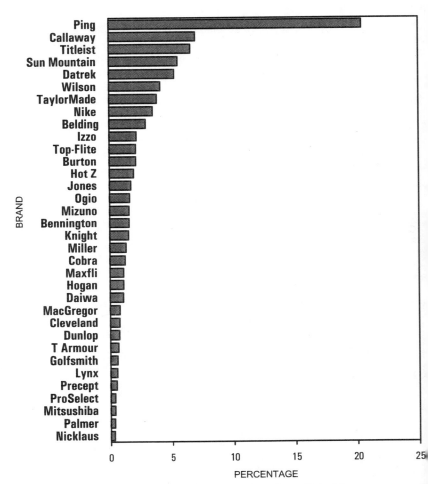

Percentage share of consumer equipment in use. Nationwide on-course consumer survey conducted summer 2003; 3,283 respondents.

More than one in five U.S. consumer golf bags in use are **Ping**.

Clubmakers Callaway and Titleist are the second and third most popular bag brands, followed by bag specialist Sun Mountain, which manufactures some of the clubmakers' name-brand bags.

BAGS: WHAT CONSUMERS USE MOST

Consumer Bag Usage by Size

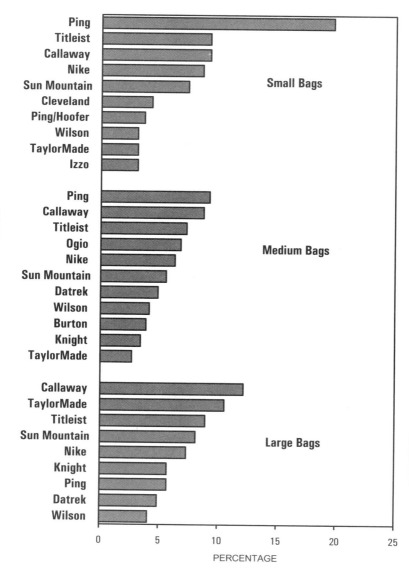

Bags

Consumer Usage

Percentage share of consumer equipment in use. Nationwide on-course consumer survey conducted summer 2004; 3,283 respondents.

BAGS: WHAT CONSUMERS USE MOST

Bag Brand Usage by Handicap

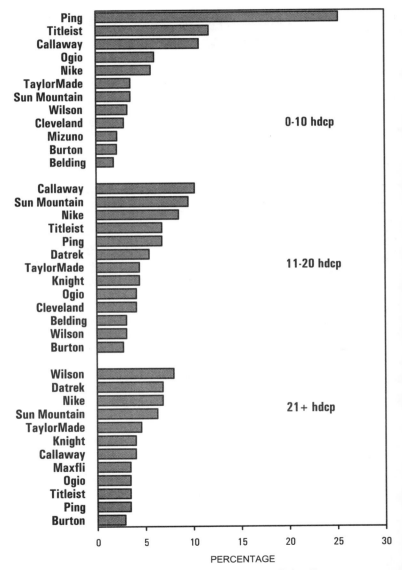

Percentage share of consumer equipment in use. Nationwide on-course consumer survey conducted summer 2003; 3,283 respondents.

BAGS: WHAT CONSUMERS USE MOST

Bag Brand Usage by Age

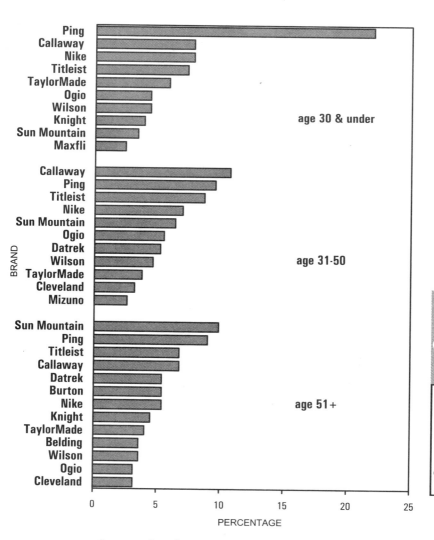

Percentage share of consumer equipment in use. Nationwide on-course consumer survey conducted summer 2003; 3,283 respondents.

U.S. consumers use a wide array of golf bags, with low-handicap and younger golfers preferring Ping.

Darrell Golfer Satisfaction Ratings™
Bag Brands by Handicap

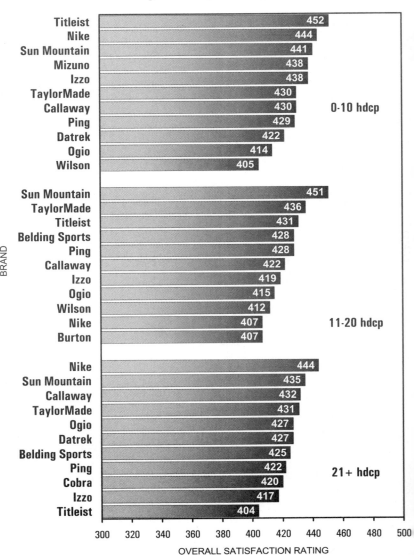

BRAND

0-10 hdcp

Titleist	452
Nike	444
Sun Mountain	441
Mizuno	438
Izzo	438
TaylorMade	430
Callaway	430
Ping	429
Datrek	422
Ogio	414
Wilson	405

11-20 hdcp

Sun Mountain	451
TaylorMade	436
Titleist	431
Belding Sports	428
Ping	428
Callaway	422
Izzo	419
Ogio	415
Wilson	412
Nike	407
Burton	407

21+ hdcp

Nike	444
Sun Mountain	435
Callaway	432
TaylorMade	431
Ogio	427
Datrek	427
Belding Sports	425
Ping	422
Cobra	420
Izzo	417
Titleist	404

OVERALL SATISFACTION RATING

300   320   340   360   380   400   420   440   460   480   500

"How satisfied are you with your equipment?" 500 is most satisfied. 100 is least satisfied. Consumer golfers rate the equipment they are actually using the day of the survey. 2,266 opinion respondents. (Minimum of 12 responses per subgroup for brands shown.)

BAGS: CONSUMER OPINIONS

Darrell Golfer Satisfaction Ratings™
Bag Brands by Age

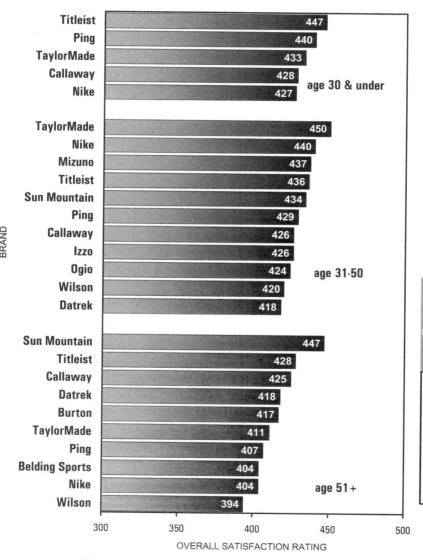

"How satisfied are you with your equipment?" 500 is most satisfied. 100 is least satis-fied. Consumer golfers rate the equipment they are actually using the day of the survey. 2,266 opinion respondents. (Minimum of 12 responses per subgroup for brands shown.)

Bags

Consumer Opinions

Darrell Golfer Satisfaction Ratings™
Bag Brands by Feature

—— Satisfaction SCORE by Equipment Feature ——

BAGS *(Listed Alphabetically)*	Overall	Value	Weight	Design Features
Average Score	*420*	*425*	*416*	*419*
Belding Sports	410	414	402	412
Bennington	412	425	406	412
Burton	400	409	394	404
Callaway	*428*	433	424	428
Cleveland	*442*	*458*	*437*	*437*
Cobra	423	429	413	419
Datrek	417	425	410	417
Hogan	395	395	389	405
Izzo	426	434	426	415
Knight	414	422	416	416
MacGregor	374	379	358	374
Maxfli	*428*	436	*436*	436
Mizuno	423	421	409	417
Nike	427	429	*436*	432
Ogio	417	409	402	417
Ping	427	427	427	426
Spalding	412	412	404	404
Sun Mountain	*442*	*447*	*448*	*437*
Tommy Armour	416	*453*	422	*439*
TaylorMade	*433*	*440*	425	*438*
Titleist	*437*	438	428	*440*
Wilson	402	420	399	398

"How satisfied are you with your equipment?" 500 is most satisfied. 100 is least satisfied. Consumer golfers rate the equipment they are actually using the day of the survey. 2,266 opinion respondents. (Minimum of 15 responses per subgroup for brands shown.)

❖ Compare each score to the average seen in the top row.
❖ Numbers in *bold italic* indicate top 5 scores in each category.

Sun Mountain, Cleveland and Titleist bags score the highest overall satisfaction scores from consumers who use them.

Sometimes brands that are not widely used receive extremely high usage scores. This indicates a small but staunchly loyal base of supporters for the brand.

Tour - Bag Affiliation by Brand

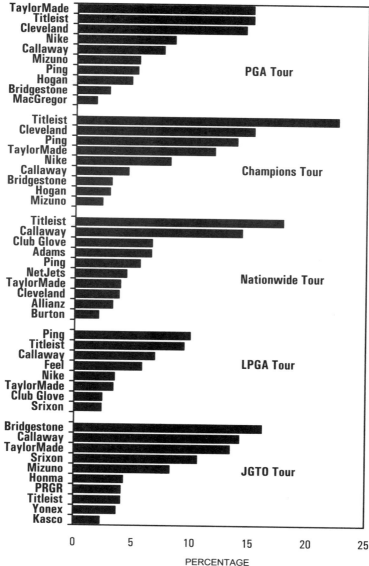

2003 Complete Season.

PGA Tour - Bag Affiliation
Overall vs. Winners

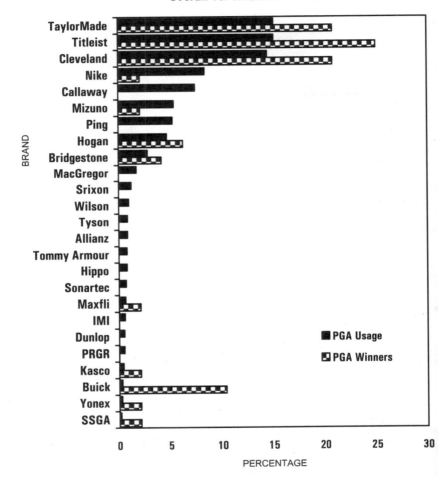

All 2003 PGA Tournaments. Sample size: 6,503 players; 48 winners.
Every brand used to win a tournament is on this chart

All other bag brands used on PGA Tour in 2003: **Adams, Administaff, Arrigo Dodgeland, Badds, Barry Evans, Belding, Best Buy, Bluegreen, Budweiser, Cingular, Ciris, Club Glove, Credit Suisse, Davey, David Frost, Dimension, Fairfield, Faldo, Feel, GM, GM Card, Golfdom, Hartford, Heniz, Henry-Griffitts, Heritage, Hughes, Hyatt, Inesis, La Jolla, Las Vegas Golf, Las Vegas Lake, Lexmark, Lloyds, Lynx, M Golf, Maverick, Michelob, Mills Pride, Natural Golf, Netjets, Next, Nicklaus, Ogio, Orlimar, Penley, Pioneer, Polo, Reese`s, Sap, SBC, Seaforth, Slazenger, Software Tag, Spring, Sun Mountain, Toyota, US Kids, USA, Vulcan, Whitten Lazer Eye, Yes, Zuma Beach.**

BAGS: PRO USAGE

Champions Tour - Bag Affiliation
Overall vs. Winners

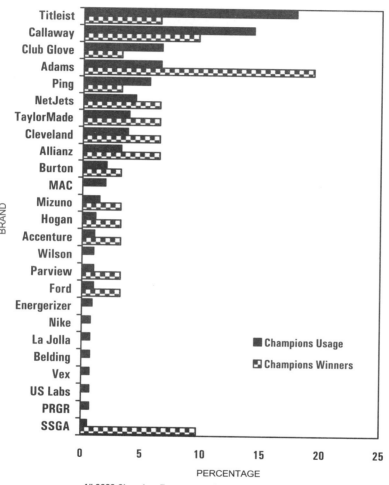

All 2003 Champions Tournaments. Sample size: 2,605 players; 31 winners.
Every brand used to win a tournament is on this chart.

All other bag brands used on Champions Tour in 2003: **AC Delco, Accuflex, Bridgestone, Club Car, Cobra, Eagle Flight, Fairfield, Golf Gear, Golf Psych, Golf USA, Golfsmith, Goodwrench, Grupo Libra, Henry-Griffitts, Honma, Hyatt, Kasco, KZG, Lynx, Michelob, Miller, My IQ, NBC Sports, Next, Nicklaus, None, Oak Tree, O'Doul`s, PDC, PGA Tour, Power Arc, Powerbilt, Putting Peg, Royal, SDGA, Seaforth, Simplot, Special Olympics, Srixon, Sun Mountain, Teamo, The Hamptons, The Villages, Tommy Armour, Top-Flite, Tour Edge, Troon, True Temper, US Kids, Vanderbilt, Winn, Yonex.**

Nationwide Tour - Bag Affiliation
Overall vs. Winners

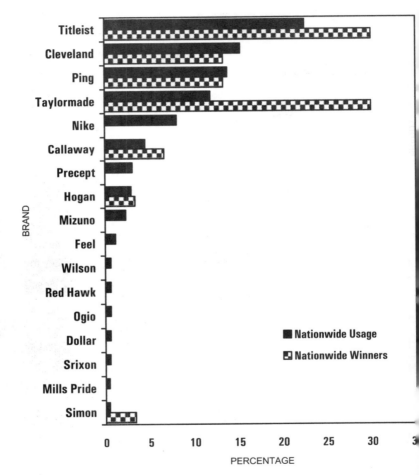

All 2003 Nationwide Tournaments. Sample size: 4,476 players; 30 winners.
Every brand used to win a tournament is on this chart. All other bag brands used on Nationwide Tour in 2003,
Accuflex, Administaff, Advantage, Albatross, Apache, Arrigo Dodgeland, Belding, Burton, CCM, Club
Glove, Dunlop, Earthlink, Ford, Gateway, Gentle White, Golfap.Com, Golfdom, Henry-Griffitts, Holden,
Hotz, Hughes, Izzo, Kasco, MacGregor, Maxfli, Mutual Omaha, Nicklaus, Oakley, Penley, PRGR,
Prosimmon, Ricoh, SAAS Seaforth, Silver Springs, Sonartec, Spring, Straightdown, Strata, Sun
Mountain, Sunpak, Swing Sync, Tommy Armour, Tommy Bahama, Tour Edge, Town & Country, Toyota,
Tyson, US Kids, US Kids Golf, UST, Vulcan, Zuma Beach.

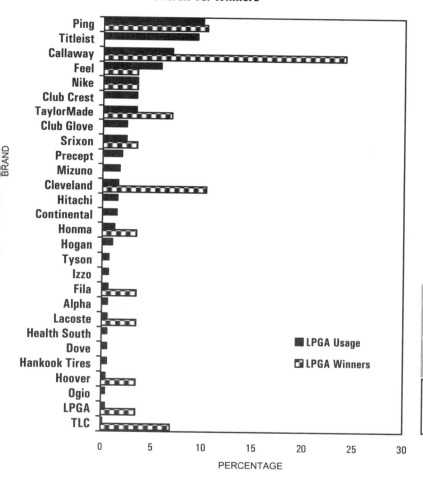

LPGA Tour - Bag Affiliation
Overall vs. Winners

All 2003 LPGA Tournaments. Sample size: 3,857 players; 29 winners. Every brand used to win a tournament is on this chart.

All other bag brands used on LPGA Tour in 2003; *Astra, Birds Eye, Canon, Daks, Davey, DSW, E Lord, Heniz, Henry-Griffitts, JAL, Jones, Kasco, L.F., Lopez, M Golf, Makser, Maxfli, Montech, New Zealand, Oakley, Odyssey, Onoff, Orlimar, Penley, S Yard, Snoopy, Sun Mountain, USGA, Wilson, Yonex.*

Aided by Annika Sörenstam's victories, Callaway leads in bag winners.

Japan Tour - Bag Affiliation
Overall vs. Winners

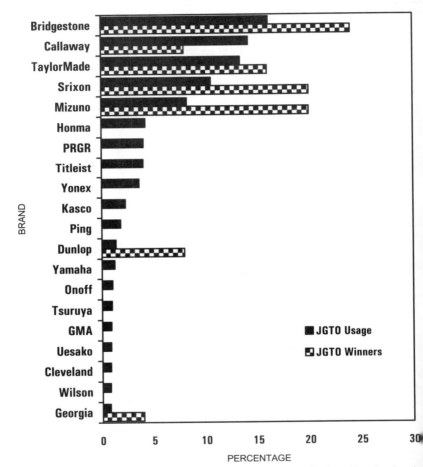

All 2003 JGTO Tournaments. Sample size: 3,342 players; 25 winners. Every brand used to win a tournament is on this chart.

All other bag brands used on JGTO Tour in 2003; **Adidas, Buick, Crews, Daiwa, Daks, Descente, Evisu Feel, Fourteen, Gauge Design, Grand Prix, Graphite Design, Hogan, Le Coq, MacGregor, Maruman Munsingwear, Nicon, Nike, Nikon, Oakley, Pearly Gates, Puma, Royal Collection, S Yard, The Major Tour Concept, Vex.**

Bridgestone, Callaway, TaylorMade, Srixon and Mizuno bags are highly visible on the Japan Golf Tour.

2003 Tournament Winners

Tour	Player	2003 Tournament Wins	Affiliation (Bag)
PGA	Appleby, Stuart	Las Vegas Invitational	Bridgestone
	Armour III, Tommy	Valero Texas Open	Titleist
	Campbell, Chad	The Tour Championship Presented by Coca-Cola	Cleveland
	Clarke, Darren	WGC -- NEC Invitational	TaylorMade
	Couples, Fred	Shell Houston Open	TaylorMade
	Crane, Ben	BellSouth Classic	Titleist
	Curtis, Ben	The Open Championship	Titleist
	Els, Ernie	Mercedes Championships	Titleist
		Sony Open	Titleist
	Flesch, Steve	HP Classic of New Orleans	Cleveland
	Furyk, Jim	U.S. Open Championship	Hogan
		Buick Open	Hogan
	Goosen, Retief	Chrysler Championship	TaylorMade
	Hoch, Scott	Ford Championship at Doral	Yonex
	Huston, John	Southern Farm Bureau Classic	Maxfli
	Jacobsen, Peter	Greater Hartford Open	Titleist
	Kaye, Jonathan	Buick Classic	Cleveland
	Leonard, Justin	Honda Classic	Hogan
	Lewis, J.L.	84 Lumber Classic of Pennsylvania	TaylorMade
	Lickliter II, Frank	Chrysler Classic of Tuscon	Titleist
		The International	Titleist
	Love III, Davis	AT&T Pebble Beach National Pro-Am (Pro)	Titleist
		The Players Championship	Titleist
		MCI Heritage	Titleist
	Maruyama, Shigeki	Chrysler Classic of Greensboro	Bridgestone
	Micheel, Shaun	PGA Championship	Cleveland
	Perry, Kenny	Bank of America Colonial	TaylorMade
		Memorial Tournament	TaylorMade
		Greater Milwaukee Open	TaylorMade
	Sabbatini, Rory	FBR Capital Open	Nike
	Scott, Adam	Deutsche Bank U.S. Championship	Titleist
	Singh, Vijay	Phoenix Open	Cleveland
		EDS Byron Nelson Classic	Cleveland
		John Deere Classic	Cleveland

Bags

Tour

2003 Tournament Winners

Tour	Player	2003 Tournament Wins	Affiliation (Bag)
PGA	Stadler, Craig	BC Open	SSGA
	Toms, David	Wachovia Championship	Cleveland
		FedEx St. Jude Classic	Cleveland
	Triplett, Kirk	Reno-Tahoe Open	Kasco
	Tway, Bob	Bell Canadian Open	Mizuno
	Weir, Mike	Bob Hope Chrysler Classic	TaylorMade
		Nissan Open	TaylorMade
		The Masters	TaylorMade
	Woods, Tiger	Buick Invitational	Buick
		WGC -- Accenture Consulting Match Play Championships	Buick
		Bay Hill Invitational Presented by Cooper Tires	Buick
		100th Western Open	Buick
		WGC -- American Express Championship	Buick
Champions	Ahern, Jim	Music City Championship at Gaylord Opryland	Ford
	Barr, Dave	Royal Caribbean Classic	Titleist
	Davis, Rodger	Toshiba Senior Classic	Burton
	Doyle, Allen	FleetBoston Classic	Adams
	Eger, David	Mastercard Classic	Titleist
	Fernandez, Vicente	ACE Group Classic	Allianz
	Fleisher, Bruce	Verizon Classic	Callaway
	Gilder, Bob	Emerald Coast Classic	Ping
	Hatalsky, Morris	Columbus Southern Open	Cleveland
	Irwin, Hale	Kinko`s Classic of Austin	TaylorMade
		Turtle Bay Championship	TaylorMade
	Jacobs, John	Senior PGA Championship	Netjets
	Jenkins, Tom	Bruno`s Memorial Classic	Parview
	Levi, Wayne	3M Championship	No Affl
	Lietzke, Bruce	Liberty Mutual Legends of Golf	Adams
		U.S. Senior Open	Adams
	Morgan, Gil	Kroger Classic	Club Glove

2003 Tournament Winners

Tour	Player	2003 Tournament Wins	Affiliation (Bag)
Champions	Nelson, Larry	Constellation Energy Classic	Adams
	Pooley, Don	Allianz Championship	Cleveland
	Purtzer, Tom	SBC Classic	Mizuno
	Quigley, Dana	MasterCard Championship	Allianz
	Sigel, Jay	Bayer Advantage Invitational	Accenture
	Stadler, Craig	Ford Senior Players Championship	SSGA
		Greater Hickory Classic at Rock Barn	SSGA
		SBC Championship	SSGA
	Tewell, Doug	Farmers Charity Classic	Netjets
	Thorpe, Jim	Long Island Classic	Callaway
		Charles Schwab Cup Championship	Callaway
	Watson, Tom	Senior British Open	Adams
		JELD-WEN Tradition	Adams
	Weibring, D.A.	SAS Championship	Hogan
Nationwide	Bohn, Jason	Chattanooga Classic	Titleist
	Boros, Guy	Lake Erie Charity Classic	Taylormade
		Dayton Open	Taylormade
	Bowden, Craig	Miccosukee Championship	Simon
	Brigman, D.J.	Permian Basin Charity Golf Classic	Ping
	Carter, Tom	Samsung Canadian PGA Championship	TaylorMade
		Price Cutter Charity Classic	TaylorMade
		Alberta Calgary Classic	TaylorMade
	Couch, Chris	Oregon Classic	Cleveland
		Nationwide Tour Championship	Cleveland
	Glover, Lucas	Gila River Classic	Titleist
	Gutschewski, Scott	Monterey Peninsula Classic	Cleveland
	Hensby, Mark	Henrico County Open	Ping
	Isenhour, Tripp	BMW Charity Pro-Am at the Cliffs	Taylormade
	Johnson, Zach	Rheem Classic	Titleist
		Envirocare Utah Classic	Titleist

2003 Tournament Winners

Tour	Player	2003 Tournament Wins	Affiliation (Bag)
Nationwide	Klauk, Jeff	Preferred Health Systems Wichita Open	Titleist
	Long, Michael	Virginia Beach Open	Hogan
	Mccallister, Blaine	NE Pennsylvania Classic	Titleist
	Morland IV, David	SAS Carolina Classic	TaylorMade
	Ogilvie, Joe	Jacob's Creek Open Championship	TaylorMade
		The Reese's Cup Classic	TaylorMade
	Oh, James	Mark Christopher Charity Classic	Callaway
	Palmer, Ryan	Clearwater Classic	Titleist
	Purdy, Ted	First Tee Arkansas Classic	Ping
	Stolz, Andre	LaSalle Bank Open	Callaway
	Tambellini, Roger	Albertson's Boise Open	Titleist
	Taylor, Vaughn	Knoxville Open	Ping
	Van Der Walt, Tjaart	Omaha Classic	Titleist
	Wetterich, Brett	Chitimacha Louisiana Open	Cleveland
LPGA	Alfredsson, Helen	Longs Drug Challenge	TaylorMade
	Daniel, Beth	BMO Financial Group Canadian Women's Open	No Affiliation
	Delasin, Dorothy	Mobile LPGA Tournament of Champions	Ping
	Doolan, Wendy	Welch's + Fry's Championship	Various
	Gustafson, Sophie	Samsung World Championship	Feel
	Han, Hee-Won	Sybase Big Apple Classic	
		Wendy's Championship for Children	Fila
	Inkster, Juli	LPGA Corning Classic	Various
		Evian Masters	Various
	Jones, Rosie	Asahi Ryokuken International Championship	LPGA Honma

2003 TOURNAMENT WINNERS

2003 Tournament Winners

Tour	Player	2003 Tournament Wins	Affiliation (Bag)
LPGA	Kung, Candie	LPGA Takefuji Classic	Cleveland
		Wachovia LPGA Classic hosted by Betsy King	Cleveland
		State Farm Classic	Cleveland
	Lunke, Hilary	U.S. Women`s Open	Ping
	Mallon, Meg	ADT Championship	Hoover
	Meunier-Lebouc, Patricia	Kraft Nabisco Championship	La Coste
	Pak, Se Ri	Safeway Ping	TLC
		Chick-fil-A Charity Championship	TLC
		Jamie Farr Kroger Classic	TaylorMade
	Park, Grace	Michelob Light Open at Kingsmill	Nike
	Sorenstam, Annika	Office Depot Championship Hosted by Amy Alcott	Callaway
		Kellogg Keebler Classic	Callaway
		McDonald`s LPGA Championship	Callaway
		Weetabix Women`s British Open	Callaway
		Safeway Classic	Callaway
	Stanford, Angela	ShopRite LPGA Classic	Ping
	Teske, Rachel	Giant Eagle LPGA Classic	Callaway
		Wegmans Rochester International	Callaway
	Webb, Karrie	John Q. Hammons Hotel Classic	Srixon
JGTO	Bjorn, Thomas	Dunlop Phoenix	Srixon
	Fukabori, Keiichiro	Japan Open	Georgia
	Hamilton, Todd	Fuji Sankei Classic	Mizuno
		Diamond Cup Tournament	Mizuno
		Gateway to the Mizuno Open	Mizuno
	Hoshino, Hidemasa	The Crowns	Srixon
	Imai, Katsumune	Casio World Open	TaylorMade

2003 Tournament Winners

Tour	Player	2003 Tournament Wins	Affiliation (Bag)
JGTO	Izawa, Toshimitsu	Japan Golf Tour Championship	Bridgestone
		Wood One Open Hiroshima	Bridgestone
	Jones, Brendan	Sun-Chlorella Classic	TaylorMade
	Katayama, Shingo	Japan PGA Championship	Dunlop
		ABC Championship	Dunlop
	Kawahara, Nozomi	Georgia Tokai Classic	TaylorMade
	Miyamoto, Katsumasa	Sato Foods NST Nigata Open	Bridgestone
	Miyase, Hirofumi	Tsuruya Open	Srixon
		Munsingwear Open KSB Cup	Srixon
	Murota, Kiyoshi	Mitsui Sumitomo Visa Taiheiyo Masters	TaylorMade
	Ozaki, Joe	Bridgestone Open	Bridgestone
	Randhawa, Jyoti	Suntory Open	Mizuno
	Stolz, Andre	Token Homemate Cup	Callaway
	Tajima, Soshi	Hisamitsu KBC Augusta	Srixon
	Tanihara, Hideto	Mandom Lucido Yomiuri Open	Bridgestone
	Teshima, Taichi	Aiful Cup	Mizuno
	Tomori, Katsuyoshi	JCB Classic Sendai	Bridgestone
	Yeh, Wei-Tze	ANA Open	Callaway

GLOVES

Chapter 8

GLOVES: OVERVIEW AND TRENDS

FootJoy and **Titleist** brand gloves are the leaders in U.S. consumer usage, with consistent results and loyal customers over time. But over the past couple of years, they've been joined by some new gloves on the block, **Nike** and **Maxfli**.

While FootJoy gloves are popular with golfers of all ages and abilities, Titleist gloves are used most by more frequent, more skilled consumers—a reflection of the brand's popularity among pro golfers. Nike gloves, as one might expect, are more popular with golfers under the age of 40 *(see page 207)*.

In GOLFER SATISFACTION RATINGS, the overall **top-rated brands** are MasterGrip, FootJoy, Titleist, Callaway and Nike (see pages *208 to 210*). Etonic and Kasco gloves also get high scores for **value**.

Pros on the **U.S. Tours** use FootJoy and Titleist most, with the two sister brands accounting for more than half the gloves on the PGA Tour. Other top gloves on Tour are Callaway, Nike, Bridgestone, Hogan, Maxfli, Wilson and Srixon.

The leading glove on the Japan Golf Tour? Callaway. *(See page 215.)*

What are the **top five** reasons consumers choose their new glove? 1. Good value, 2. the fit, 3. the feel, 4. brand loyalty, and 5. because the old one wore out, according to our latest nationwide survey.

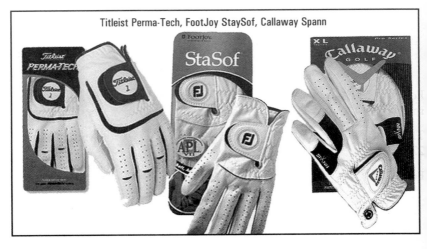

Titleist Perma-Tech, FootJoy StaySof, Callaway Spann

Consumer Glove Usage

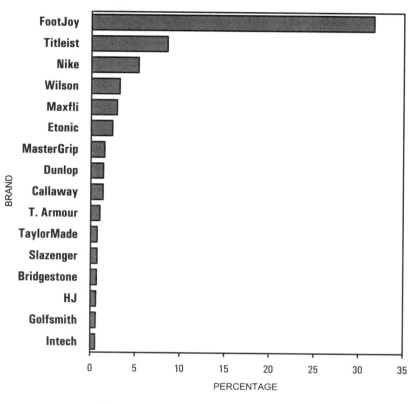

Percentage share of consumer equipment in use. Nationwide on-course consumer survey conducted summer 2003; 3,185 respondents

FootJoy gloves are far and away the top choice of consumer golfers in the U.S. One-third of all players surveyed were wearing FootJoy.

This graph shows usage among *all golfers* we surveyed, including the 27% of players who weren't using a glove.

FootJoy's share of glove-wearing golfers is 43%.

Gloves

Consumer Usage

Glove Usage by Handicap

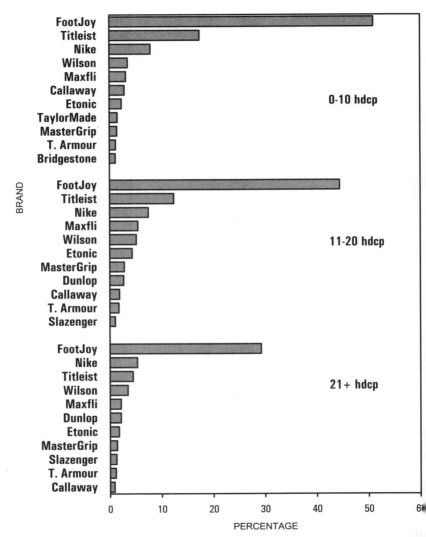

Percentage share of consumer equipment in use. Nationwide on-course consumer survey conducted summer 2003; 3,185 respondents.

FootJoy is most popular among lower-handicap players.

Glove Usage by Age

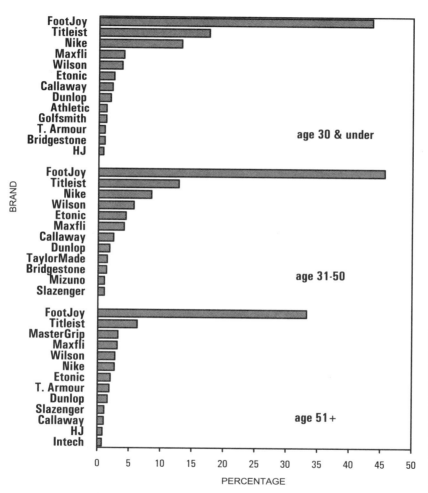

Percentage share of consumer equipment in use. Nationwide on-course consumer survey conducted summer 2003; 3,185 respondents.

FootJoy is used by nearly half of all younger consumers surveyed and is followed by Titleist in all age groups.

Nike ranks third among young to middle-aged players while MasterGrip, Maxfli and Wilson follow among older golfers.

Gloves

Consumer Usage

Darrell Golfer Satisfaction Ratings™
Glove Brands by Handicap

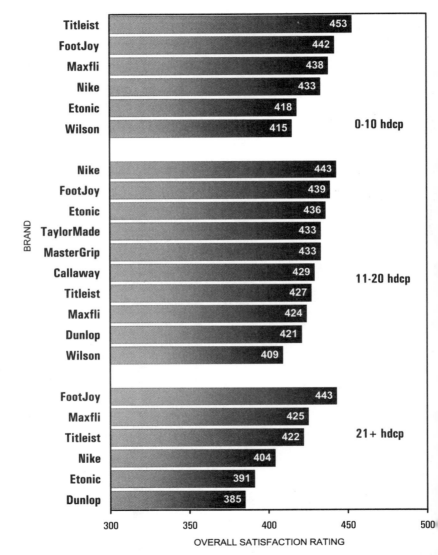

"How satisfied are you with your equipment?" 500 is most satisfied. 100 is least satisfied.
Consumer golfers rate the equipment they are actually using the day of the survey.
3,278 opinion respondents. (Minimum of 15 responses per subgroup for brands/models shown.)

GLOVES: CONSUMER OPINIONS

Darrell Golfer Satisfaction Ratings™
Glove Brands by Age

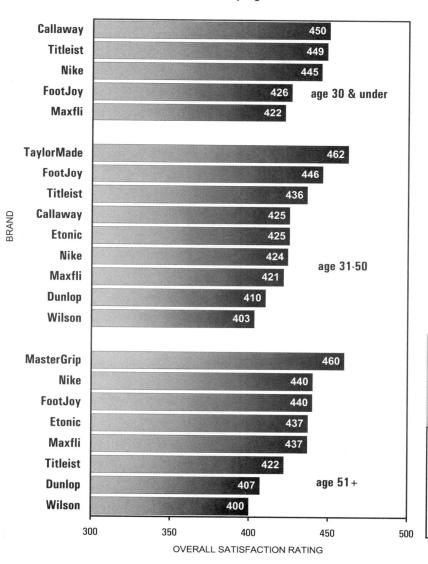

How satisfied are you with your equipment?" 500 is most satisfied. 100 is least satisfied.
3,278 opinion respondents. (Minimum of 15 responses per subgroup for brands/models
shown.)

GLOVES: CONSUMER OPINIONS

Darrell Golfer Satisfaction Ratings™
Glove Brands by Feature

—— Satisfaction SCORE by Equipment Feature ——

GLOVES

(*Listed Alphabetically*)	Overall	Fit	Value	Feel	Appearance	Durability
Average Score	*432*	*440*	*430*	*440*	*436*	*423*
Callaway	435	*462*	426	*459*	*447*	*441*
Dunlop	404	404	411	411	404	389
Etonic	420	435	433	438	431	408
FootJoy	*440*	*448*	433	*447*	445	430
• FootJoy Sta-Sof	*448*	*456*	*435*	*457*	*454*	*439*
• FootJoy WeatherSof	*454*	*462*	*435*	*462*	*458*	*442*
• FootJoy Dry ICE	421	436	414	443	443	414
Intech	383	400	400	375	362	377
Kasco	431	*477*	*454*	446	415	415
MasterGrip	*451*	*457*	*460*	*457*	*449*	*449*
Maxfli	431	435	*435*	437	432	417
Mizuno	429	429	429	441	429	429
Nike	434	437	429	439	441	428
T. Armour	406	412	406	412	406	412
TaylorMade	437	429	432	436	432	*432*
Titleist	*438*	*448*	430	*447*	*447*	430
USA	383	400	417	392	375	383
Wilson	408	420	422	417	406	400

"How satisfied are you with your equipment?" 500 is most satisfied. 100 is least satisfied. 3,278 opinion respondents. Scores based on a minimum of fifteen responses per brand.

❖ Compare each score to the average seen in the top row.
❖ Numbers in ***bold italic*** indicate top 5 brand scores in each category.

Mastergrip, **FootJoy** and **Titleist** are three glove brands receiving high satisfaction ratings from consumer golfers.

Callaway, Kasco and **Maxfli** also receive top ratings for one or more glove features.

We have broken out some of the more popular models of the industry leader **FootJoy**: Sta-Sof, WeatherSof and Dry I.C.E. Each of these models has more than the required sample size to appear in the chart.

PGA Tour - Glove Usage
Overall vs. Winners

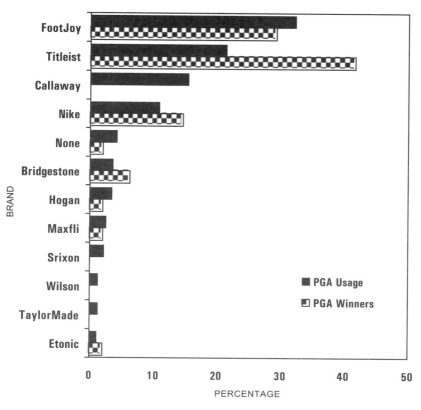

All 2003 PGA Tournaments. Sample size: 6,503 players; 48 winners.
Every brand used to win a tournament is on this chart.
All other glove brands used on PGA Tour in 2003; Gluv, Master Grip, Mizuno, Nicklaus,
Norman, PRGR, Slazenger.

While **FootJoy** is the most popular glove on the PGA Tour in 2003, its sister brand **Titleist** captures the most wins.

The brand shares of glove and ball usage *(see p. 22)* show some correlation as tour players often match their glove to their ball.

Champions Tour - Glove Usage
Overall vs. Winners

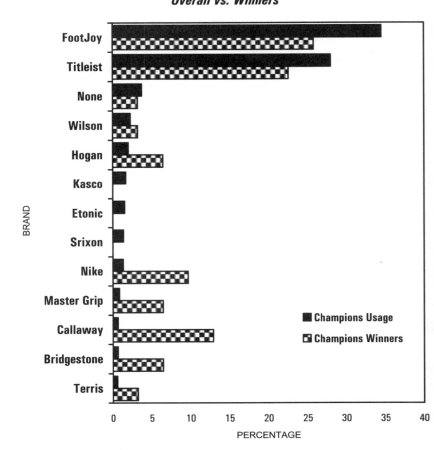

All 2003 Champions Tournaments. Sample size: 2,605 players; 31 winners.
Every brand used to win a tournament is on this chart. All other glove brands used on
Champions Tour in 2003: Gluv, Lynx, Maxfli, Mizuno, Nicklaus, Ping, PRGR,
Slazenger, TayloMade, Thorpie, Vex.

FootJoy and co-brand **Titleist** lead the seniors in both glove usage and wins in 2003.

Nine different brands notch victories on the 2003 Champions Tour; one winner went gloveless.

Nationwide Tour - Glove Usage
Overall vs. Winners

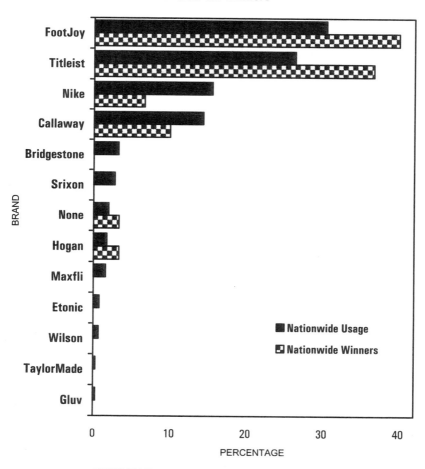

All 2003 PGA Tournaments. Sample size: 6,503 players; 48 winners.
Every brand used to win a tournament is on this chart.
All other glove brands used on PGA Tour in 2003; Club Crest, Gluv, Master Grip,
Mizuno, Nicklaus, Norman, PRGR, Slazenger.

FootJoy, Titleist, Nike and **Callaway** gloves lead the Nationwide Tour in usage and victories.

The Callaway glove scores many more wins on the Nationwide Tour than on the PGA Tour in 2003 *(see p. 219.)*

LPGA Tour - Glove Usage
Overall vs. Winners

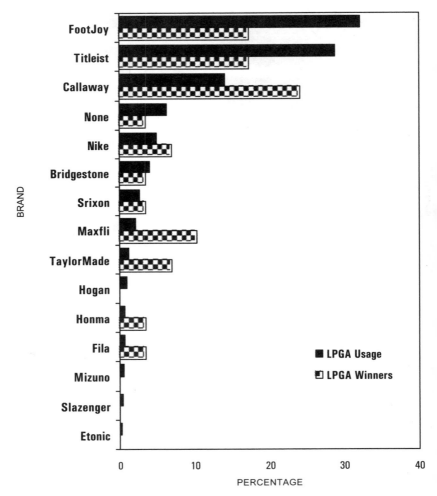

All 2003 LPGA Tournaments. Sample size: 3,857 players; 29 winners.
Every brand used to win a tournament is on this chart.
All other glove brands used on LPGA Tour in 2003: Daks, E Lord, Kasco, Lopez,
Makser, Wilson, Yonex.

FootJoy and **Titleist** gloves lead in usage on the LPGA Tour in 2003—but Callaway captures the most wins.

Japan Tour - Glove Usage
Overall vs. Winners

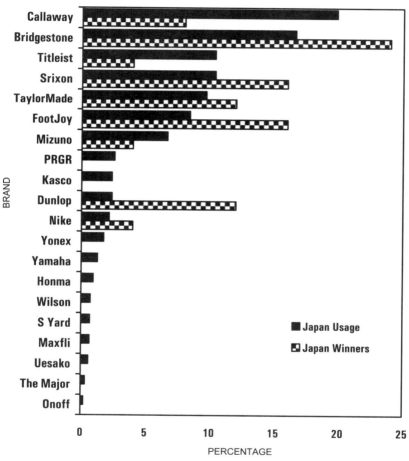

All 2003 JGTO Tournaments. Sample size: 3,342 players; 25 winners.
Every brand used to win a tournament is on this chart. All other glove brands used on
JGTO Tour in 2003: Adidas, Daiwa, Etonic, GMA, Hogan, MacGregor, Maruman,
Matsuura, Ping, Tour Concept, Vex.

While Callaway is the most popular glove brand on the Japan Golf Tour in 2003, Bridgestone contributes to the most victories.

The Japanese brands Dunlop and Srixon are much more prominent on the Japan Tour than on the U.S. Tours *(see pp. 219-222.)*

SHOES

Chapter 9

As it has been for decades, the **FootJoy** golf shoe is the top choice of pros and consumers alike. With more than 53% of all the new consumer shoes surveyed this year, FootJoy has never been more popular.

FootJoy Classics
Dry Premier

Nike and **Adidas** shoes hold steady in consumer usage, while traditional brands **Etonic** and **Dexter** have fallen back *(see page opposite)*.

Bite, though still a small player, has made inroads with consumers, with models including their unusual sandal designs.

In GOLFER SATISFACTION RATINGS, Bite leads in overall satisfaction, while FootJoy receives outstanding scores from customers of their wide range of models.

FootJoy is the leading shoe on the major U.S. Tours and Japan Golf Tour, although on the LPGA Tour Adidas, Nike and Callaway all had a bigger share of winners' shoes.

Other shoes used by the pros include Ecco, Bite, Bridgestone, Etonic, Oakley, Reebok and Mizuno *(see pages 235 to 239)*.

For their spikes, the pros choose the **Softspikes** Black Widow more than any other model. The Champ Scorpion is another popular spike. One-third of PGA touring pros continue to use metal spikes *(see pages 240-241)*.

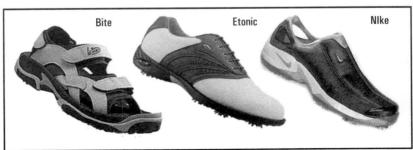

Bite   Etonic   Nike

Consumer Shoe Usage

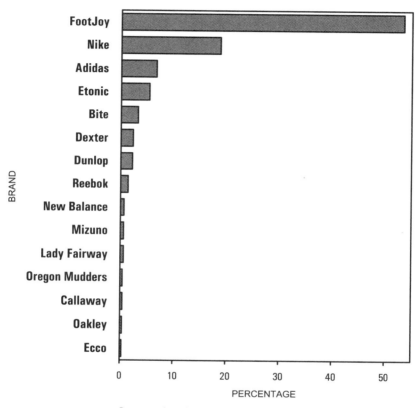

Percentage share of new consumer equipment in use. Nationwide on-course consumer survey conducted summer 2003; 3,113 respondents, 1,129 with new shoes.

Among recreational golfers in the U.S., more than half of the new shoes in use are made by FootJoy. Nike and Adidas take second and third place.

PGA Tour players wear even more FootJoys *(see page 237)*

Shoes

Consumer Usage

Shoe Usage by Handicap

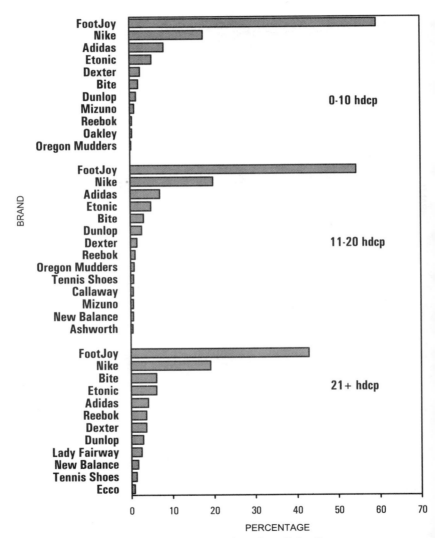

Percentage share of consumer equipment in use. Nationwide on-course consumer survey conducted summer 2003; 1,129 respondents.

Consumers' choice of shoes doesn't vary greatly by handicap group, although low-handicap players stick to the major brands more.

SHOES: WHAT CONSUMERS USE MOST

Shoe Usage by Age

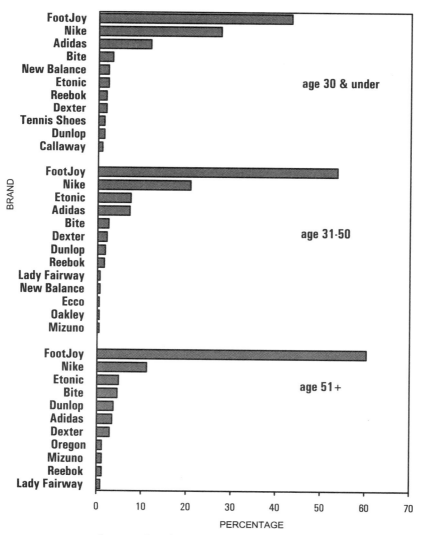

Percentage share of consumer equipment in use. Nationwide on-course consumer survey conducted summer 2003; 1,129 respondents.

Adidas and Nike golf shoes are enjoying success with younger golfers in the U.S.

Shoes

Consumer Usage

Darrell Golfer Satisfaction Ratings™
Shoe Brands by Feature

—— Satisfaction SCORE by Equipment Feature ——

SHOES

(Listed Alphabetically)	**Overall**	**Value**	**Appearance**	**Comfort**	**Durability**
Average Score	*434*	*432*	*436*	*438*	*432*
Adidas	*429*	*433*	*435*	*434*	*427*
Bite	*466*	*469*	*455*	*466*	*469*
Dexter	400	422	401	402	401
Dunlop	*432*	*436*	423	*433*	*426*
Etonic	424	425	*425*	*429*	*424*
FootJoy	*442*	*435*	*445*	*445*	*440*
Lady Fairway	*429*	*443*	421	421	421
Mizuno	404	413	404	413	417
Nike	425	419	*430*	*429*	419
Reebok	424	427	409	*429*	422

"How satisfied are you with your equipment?" 500 is most satisfied. 100 is least satisfied. Consumer golfers rate the equipment they are actually using the day of the survey. 2,056 opinion respondents. (Minimum of 15 responses per subgroup for brands/models shown.)

> ❖   Compare each score to the average seen in the top row.
> ❖   Numbers in ***bold italic*** indicate top 5 brand scores in each category.

The Darrell Golfer Satisfaction Ratings reflect the **opinions** of golfers who are actually using the equipment in question.

Bite and FootJoy shoes receive the highest overall satisfaction ratings in this year's survey.

Other brands with top satisfaction scores include Adidas, Dunlop, Etonic and Nike.

Differences of only a few points are not statistically relevant.

Darrell Golfer Satisfaction Ratings™
Shoe Brands by Handicap

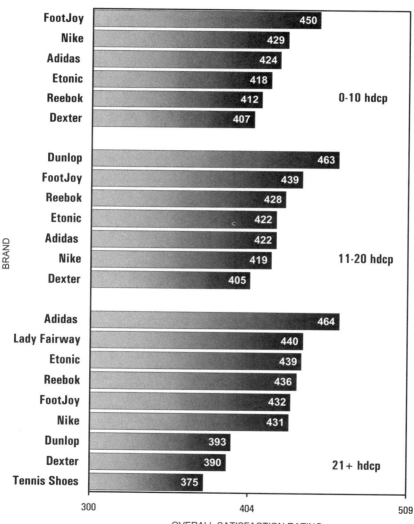

OVERALL SATISFACTION RATING

"How satisfied are you with your equipment?" 500 is most satisfied. 100 is least satisfied. 2,056 opinion respondents. (Minimum of 15 responses per subgroup for brands/models shown.)

Shoes

Consumer Opinions

Darrell Golfer Satisfaction Ratings™
Shoe Brands by Age

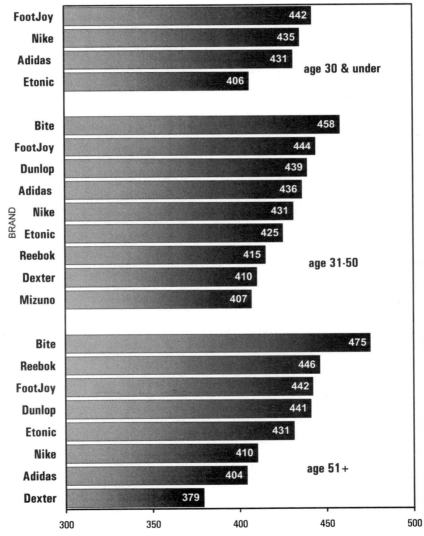

"How satisfied are you with your equipment?" 500 is most satisfied. 100 is least satisfied.
2,265 opinion respondents. (Minimum of 15 responses per subgroup for brands/models shown.)

Top Shoes at Major Amateur Events

U.S. AMATEUR
FootJoy
Adidas
Nike
Reebok
Etonic

U.S. WOMEN'S AMATEUR
FootJoy
Nike
Ecco
Etonic
New Balance

NCAA DIV. 1 MEN'S
FootJoy
Adidas
Nike
Reebok
Etonic

NCAA WOMEN'S
FootJoy
Nike
Adidas

U.S. BOYS JUNIOR
FootJoy
Adidas
Nike

U.S. GIRLS JUNIOR
FootJoy
Adidas
Nike
Ecco
Bite
Etonic

2003 Data. Listed in order of decreasing shoe brand usage at each tournament.

Shoes

Amateur Usage

Shoe me the money!

(Clockwise from top left) Dexter Women's Kiltie, Dexter Softshoe Retro, Bite Kahuna Sandal, DexterGolfMoc, Bite Power Moc, Bite Women's Slingshot, FootJoy CoolJoys, FootJoy Women's Classics, Adidas Z Traxion & Adidas Climacool.

PGA Tour - Shoe Usage
Overall vs. Winners

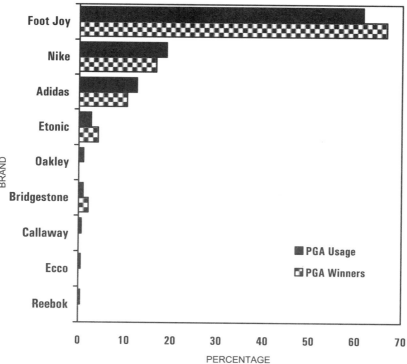

All 2003 PGA Tournaments. Sample size: 6,503 players; 48 winners.
Every brand used to win a tournament is on this chart. All other shoe brands used on PGA
*Tour in 2003: **Bite, Bally, Dunlop, MacGregor, Mizuno, Nebulon, Norman, Polo,***
Surefoot, Timing.

With more than 60% of the players wearing its shoes, **FootJoy** is the dominant brand on the PGA Tour in usage and wins.

Nike ranks second in PGA usage and victories, followed by **Adidas**.

Winners on the 2003 PGA Tour wore only five different brands of shoes.

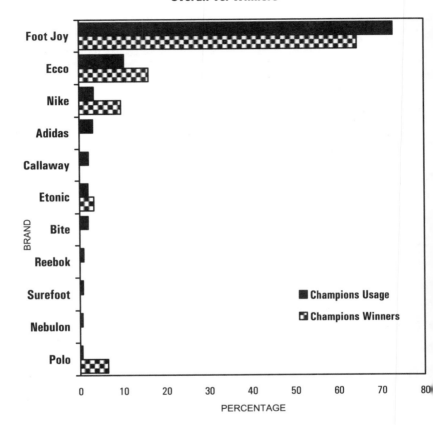

Champions Tour - Shoe Usage
Overall vs. Winners

All 2003 Champions Tournaments. Sample size: 2,605 players; 31 winners. Every brand used to win a tournament is on this chart. All other shoe brands used on Champions Tour in 2003: Asics, Dexter, Florsheim, J&M, MacGregor, Michael Toski, Mizuno, Timing, Toski, Wilson, Yonex.

FootJoy shoes rule on the Champions Tour, in usage as well as in victories.

The lesser-known Ecco shoe is number two among senior players, followed by Nike.

Nationwide Tour - Shoe Usage
Overall vs. Winners

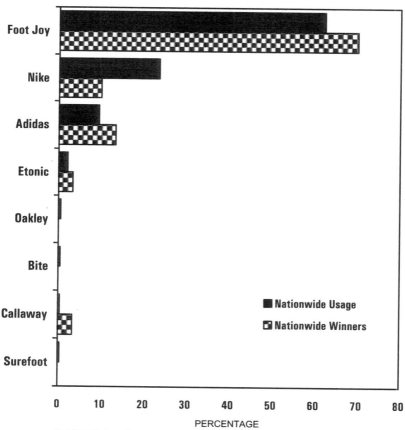

All 2003 Nationwide Tournaments. Sample size: 4,476 players; 30winners.

Every brand used to win a tournament is on this chart. All other shoe brands used on LPGA Tour in 2003: Dexter, Ecco, Florsheim, Mephisto, Mizuno, New Balance, Pro Grip, Reebok.

FootJoy, **Nike** and **Adidas** shoes are the top three brands on the Nationwide Tour in 2003.

Shoes

Tour

LPGA Tour - Shoe Usage
Overall vs. Winners

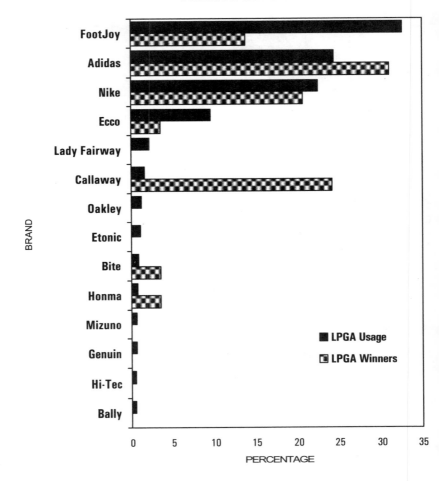

All 2003 LPGA Tournaments. Sample size: 3,857 players; 29 winners.

Every brand used to win a tournament is on this chart. All other shoe brands used on LPGA Tour in 2003: Aero Green, Ashworth, Asics, Dexter, Dunlop, E Lord, Puma, Reebok, Srixon, Surefoot, Titleist.

Although FootJoy leads the LPGA Tour in usage in 2003, Adidas captures the highest number of wins. The Callaway shoe has a very prominent winning player wearing it.

SHOES: PRO USAGE

Japan Tour - Shoe Usage
Overall vs. Winners

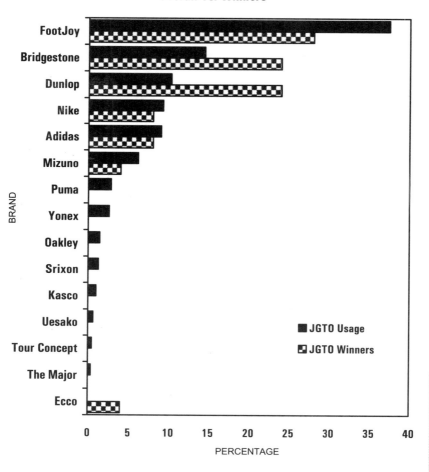

All 2003 JGTO Tournaments. Sample size: 3,342 players; 25 winners.

Every brand used to win a tournament is on this chart. All other shoe brands used on JGTO Tour in 2003: Bite, Daiwa, Etonic, Honma, Le Coq, Onoff, PRGR, Tsuruya, Wilson.

FootJoy shoes top the Japan Golf Tour. Bridgestone and Dunlop tie for second in wins.

Spikes on Tour

Softspikes' **Black Widow** is the leading spike model on the PGA, Champions, Nationwide and at major amateur tournaments again this year *(see following page)*.

Champ's Scorpion leads on the LPGA Tour, and is the second-place model on the Nationwide Tour.

Softspikes Black Widow

Champ Scorpion

The decline of the traditional **metal spike** seems to have halted, at least on the PGA Tour. With the first uptick in metal usage since the rise of the Softspike, more than one-third of PGA players are using metal spikes *(see graph, below)*.

PGA Tour Use of Metal Spikes 1996 to 2003

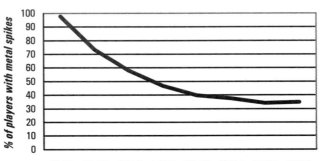

Spike Models
By Tour

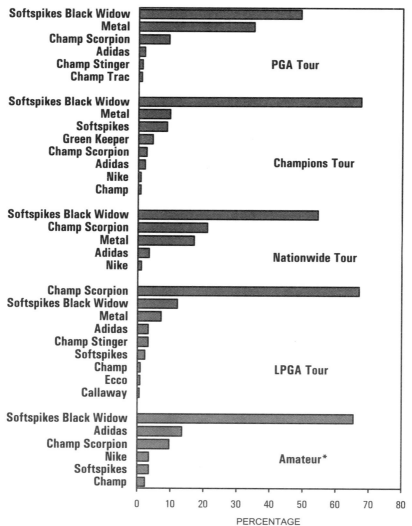

Percentage share of spikes used during 2003. Sample sizes: PGA 6,502, Champions 2,604, Nationwide 4,158, LPGA 3,725, Amateur 750.

*Amateur tournaments are NCAA Div. 1 Men's Championship, NCAA Women's, Public Links, U.S. Amateur.

Shoes

Spikes

SHIRTS

Chapter 10

SHIRTS: OVERVIEW AND TRENDS

As they have for years, more consumers wear **Ashworth** golf shirts than any other brand. **Polo by Ralph Lauren** and **Nike** round out the top three golf shirts, with Nike a special favorite of younger players *(see pages 245 & 247).*

Shirts are one of the most **diverse** areas of the golf equipment and apparel world, with the top three brands accounting for less than 30% of all golfers surveyed. *(See graph at right.)*

Topping the GOLFER SATISFACTION RATINGS for shirts are **Callaway, Tommy Hilfiger, Adidas, Cutter & Buck** and **Ping** *(see pages 248 to 250).*

2003 Consumer Shirt Usage

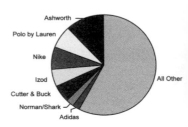

One-third of golfers surveyed bought their shirt at an on-course pro shop. A slightly higher pecentage got them at non-golf retail outlets, like department stores, while about two in ten went to off-course golf shops.

SHIRTS: WHAT CONSUMERS USE MOST

Consumer Shirt Usage

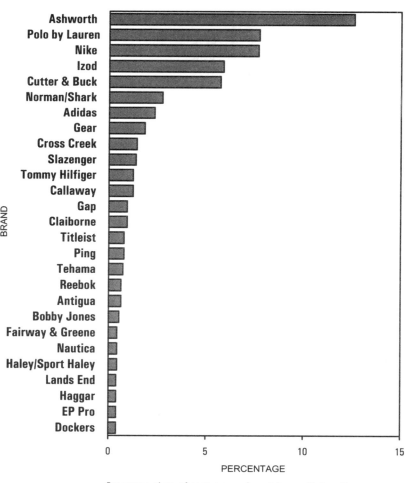

Percentage share of consumer equipment in use. Nationwide on-course consumer survey conducted summer 2003; 1,009 respondents.

More U.S. recreational players wear Ashworth golf shirts than any other brand.

Because of the wide array of shirts available, most brands have only a small percentage of the marketplace.

Shirts

Consumer Usage

Shirt Usage by Handicap

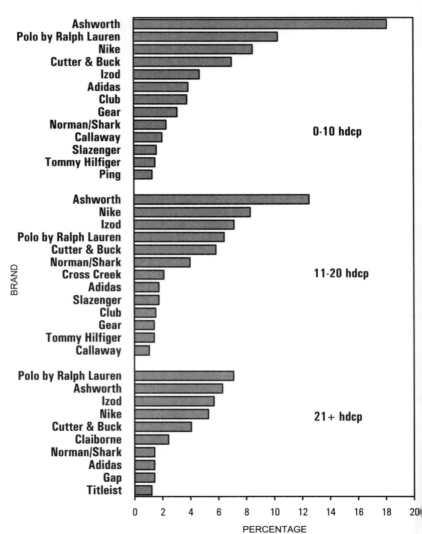

PERCENTAGE

Percentage share of consumer equipment in use. Nationwide on-course consumer survey conducted summer 2003; 1,009 respondents.

Ashworth, Polo by Ralph Lauren and Nike are the shirts worn most by low-handicap consumer golfers in the U.S.

SHIRTS: WHAT CONSUMERS USE MOST

Shirt Usage by Age

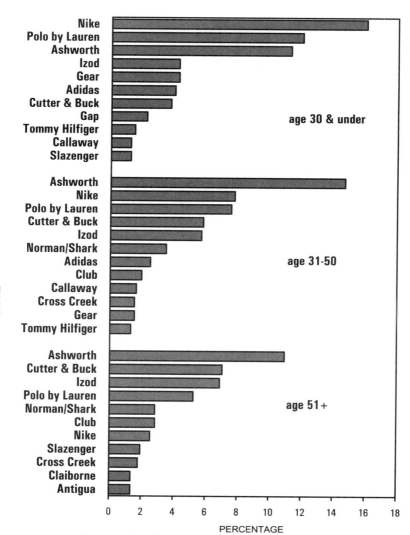

Percentage share of consumer equipment in use. Nationwide on-course consumer survey conducted summer 2003; 1,009 respondents.

Nike golf shirts have made a big impression on younger golfers, while Ashworth is popular with all ages.

Darrell Golfer Satisfaction Ratings™
Shirt Brands by Handicap

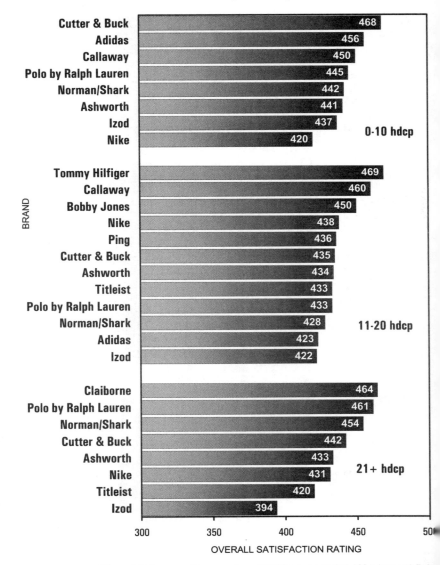

"How satisfied are you with your equipment?" 500 is most satisfied. 100 is least satisfied. Consumer golfers rate the equipment they are actually using the day of the survey. 1,455 opinion respondents. (Minimum of 12 responses per subgroup for brands shown.)

Darrell Golfer Satisfaction Ratings™
Shirt Brands by Age

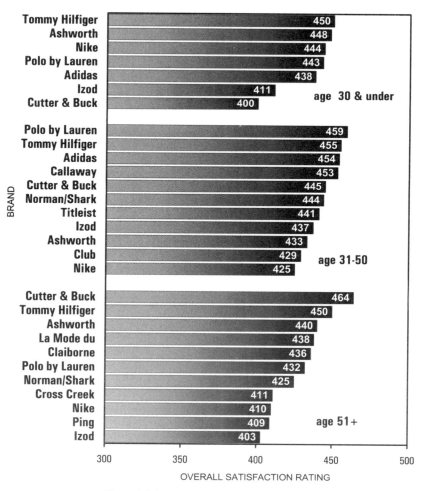

"How satisfied are you with your equipment?" 500 is most satisfied. 100 is least satisfied. Consumer golfers rate the equipment they are actually using the day of the survey. 1,455 opinion respondents. (Minimum of 12 responses per subgroup for brands shown.)

These two pages show golfers' overall satisfaction with their shirts. We see some interesting variations of opinion between golfers of different ages and abilities.

Shirts

Consumer Opinions

Darrell Golfer Satisfaction Ratings™
Shirt Brands by Feature

—— Satisfaction SCORE by Equipment Feature ——

SHIRTS

(Listed Alphabetically)	Overall	Comfort	Durability	Appearance	Value	Fit
Average Score	437	443	435	442	426	438
Adidas	*450*	*456*	444	*458*	*444*	452
Ashworth	438	444	437	448	428	439
Bobby Jones	*457*	*479*	*464*	*493*	371	*457*
Callaway	*461*	*465*	*470*	*470*	*448*	*470*
Claiborne	440	445	440	440	410	440
Cross Creek	440	440	420	447	427	*460*
Cutter & Buck	*448*	449	451	446	*440*	444
Gear	392	383	392	383	392	383
Izod	422	440	419	428	431	427
La Mode du Golf	443	448	435	438	429	443
Nike	428	427	424	431	414	428
Norman/Shark	439	449	444	451	*431*	442
Ping	446	*456*	*460*	*460*	432	448
Polo by Lauren	446	451	441	455	405	*454*
Slazenger	441	453	*453*	447	424	453
Titleist	443	454	439	457	421	443
Tommy Hilfiger	*452*	*455*	*458*	471	426	*458*

"How satisfied are you with your equipment?" 500 is most satisfied. 100 is least satisfied. Consumer golfers rate the equipment they are actually using the day of the survey. 1,455 opinion respondents. (Minimum of 12 responses per subgroup for brands shown.)

❖ Compare each score to the average seen in the top row.
❖ Numbers in *bold italic* indicate top 5 scores in each category.

The Callaway golf shirt receives the highest overall satisfaction rating in 2003, as well as in durability, value and fit. Bobby Jones is ranked best for comfort and appearance.

Other brands scoring higher in overall satisfaciton than the average score (437) are Tommy Hilfiger, Adidas, Cutter & Buck, Ping, Polo by Ralph Lauren, La Mode du Golf, Titleist, Slazenger, Claiborne, Cross Creek, Shark by Greg Norman and Ashworth.

Dressed to Swing

Survey Methodology

Consumer Usage:

The methodology of the Darrell Consumer Survey was designed in its current form in 1982 in association with the market-research authority Doss Struse, subsequently with the A.C. Nielsen Company. The methodology has been used consistently in conducting the annual survey, yielding dependable and comparable results.

Direct observation is the principal distinguishing feature of our approach. Every year, we inspect the equipment being used on courses throughout the country, including such information as the age and handicap of the golfers.

Courses are selected randomly from every region in the U.S. without regard to professional staff brand affiliations. Interviews are conducted on both private and public courses.

Because the study is designed to interview golfers on the course, the yearly sample favors frequent golfers. Frequent golfers have a greater chance of being included in the sample because they are more likely to be on the course when interviews are conducted.

Interviewers are experienced golf-oriented field investigators, with expertise in equipment identification. After they submit the completed forms, the Darrell Survey office staff inputs and codes the data. All forms are reviewed for thoroughness and accuracy, and then monitored for statistical reliability.

Consumer Opinions:

Consumer satisfaction surveys are conducted throughout the year at golf courses and driving ranges, subject to the same rigorous quality control as the annual survey. The difference between ratings of closely ranked brands and models are not statistically significant.

Professional Tour Data:

On the pro tours, the Darrell Survey reports on equipment used by every player. At the opening tee on the first day of play at every Official Money Tournament on the PGA, LPGA, Champions, Nationwide and Japan Golf Tours, a Darrell Survey representative inspects the bag of every player, reporting on club, ball, shoe, headgear, glove and bag useage.

The Darrell Survey has provided an independent and unbiased accounting of professional golf usage since the 1930s. This information is tabulated weekly and supplied to golf manufacturers.

Statistical Performance results are derived directly from PGA Tour data. Averages are less reliable for brands and models with small sample sizes.